Advance Praise for *Urban Agriculture*

David Tracey's *Urban Agriculture* is a road map to food security, to our reconnecting to the soil and the earth, even in cities, and to reclaiming our humanity as cultivators of community while we cultivate food.

— Dr. Vandana Shiva, scientist, environmental activist and
author of *Soil not Oil* and *Stolen Harvest*

David Tracey knows the urban gardening scene direct from the trenches where he has worked with community gardeners for years. In this very readable book, he talks to other experienced city farmers in Vancouver and shares with us their top-notch advice. David's background, as an environmental designer with a Masters degree in Landscape Architecture, makes his how-to chapters extremely useful to anyone who is planning to start an urban agriculture project.

— Michael Levenston, Executive Director,
City Farmer: Canada's Office of Urban Agriculture since 1978

David Tracey's *Urban Agriculture* is a delight. From sprouts to vegetables to fish to chickens its thorough, practical and inspiring. It is a call to all of us to take up shovels, sharpen them, and go to work on growing food.

— Lyle Estill, author of *Small is Possible*
and *Industrial Evolution*

In the future we will most need to grow food where most people already are. City farming and gardening is quite literally the wave of the future, and if we are to feed the world's people in the 21st century, urban agriculture will be critical. This book should be on the shelf of everyone who cares about food. But don't just leave it on the shelf, take it out into your community and get digging!

— Sharon Astyk, farmer and author of *Independence Days: A Guide to Sustainable Food Storage and Preservation* and *A Nation of Farmers*, www.scienceblogs.com/casaubonsbook

IDEAS AND DESIGNS FOR
THE NEW FOOD REVOLUTION

David Tracey

NEW SOCIETY PUBLISHERS

Cover design by Diane McIntosh.
All photos and illustrations © David Tracey.

Printed in Canada. First printing February 2011.

Paperback ISBN: 978-0-86571-694-0   eISBN: 978-1-55092-473-2

Inquiries regarding requests to reprint all or part of *Urban Agriculture*
should be addressed to New Society Publishers at the address below.

To order directly from the publishers, please call toll-free (North America)
1-800-567-6772, or order online at www.newsociety.com

Any other inquiries can be directed by mail to:

New Society Publishers
P.O. Box 189, Gabriola Island, BC V0R 1X0, Canada
(250) 247-9737

New Society Publishers' mission is to publish books that contribute in
fundamental ways to building an ecologically sustainable and just society,
and to do so with the least possible impact on the environment, in a manner
that models this vision. We are committed to doing this not just through
education, but through action. Our printed, bound books are printed on
Forest Stewardship Council-certified acid-free paper that is **100% post-
consumer recycled** (100% old growth forest-free), processed chlorine free,
and printed with vegetable-based, low-VOC inks, with covers produced
using FSC-certified stock. New Society also works to reduce its carbon
footprint, and purchases carbon offsets based on an annual audit to ensure
a carbon neutral footprint. For further information, or to browse our full list
of books and purchase securely, visit our website at: www.newsociety.com

Library and Archives Canada Cataloguing in Publication

Tracey, David
    Urban agriculture : ideas and designs for the new food revolution / David
    Tracey.

Includes index.
ISBN 0-86571-694-3.--ISBN 978-0-86571-694-0

    1. Urban agriculture. 2. Urban gardening. 3. Community gardens.
I. Title.

S494.5.U72T73 2011   635   C2011-900653-7

NEW SOCIETY PUBLISHERS
www.newsociety.com

MIX
Paper from
responsible sources
FSC
www.fsc.org   FSC™ C016245

Contents

The future of urban farming looks bright.

Introduction

The city of the future is green and delicious.

It is also creative and busy and messy and fun and beautiful — although the last two points were lost on the residents of the Vancouver waterfront neighborhood where I recently tried to lead a public meeting.

I was there to explain a proposal for a community garden that was to be tended by neighbors from a world of backgrounds. It was part of a government-funded program to help immigrants and Canadian-born residents build a more welcoming society by growing organic food together.

I figured it would be an easy sell because it was about food and came with a feel-good bonus. At least 40 percent of the gardeners were to be foreign-born (matching the population of the downtown peninsula) and all were to attend workshops on racism, intercultural communication and inclusive group governance. Behind the proposal was the idea that Vancouver's visible success as a multicultural city wasn't telling the whole story. It can take years for newcomers to Canada to feel a sense of belonging. So bringing a diverse group of immigrant and Canadian-born residents together to speak the same language — vegetables — was an experiment in social harmony. It would help transform Vancouver from a mere *multi*cultural city, where you might wave to the Punjabi neighbors whose names you can never recall, to an *inter*cultural city, where you actually know who they are and maybe even care about them because they're your friends and you're going to see them at the next block potluck or community center canning workshop or neighborhood food network meeting.

But first we needed land.

We weren't asking for much: a narrow strip of grass in a public park behind two fenced tennis courts above a much larger lawn beside the sea. The strip had space for about twenty food plots and a few fruit trees and berry bushes. Nothing that would turn back the tide of the industrial food system, but enough to support a worthy program aimed at combining the new food politics with community engagement.

Except that this particular community must have misread the notice. They acted like we'd called for community enragement. Judging by the aggressive way they strode into the room, glaring, I sensed I was in for a long night. Canadian decency meant they at least waited in turn to lambast the proposal and anyone like me who would dare support it, but it like was a tar-and-feathering without the tar and feathers. Not that they couldn't have afforded them. Condos in the towers overlooking that stretch of the water sell for more than a million dollars.

First to speak was a fifty-ish woman in jogging shoes. "How dare you come into *our* neighborhood and suggest something like this?" she demanded. "Where do *you* live anyway?"

I was about to answer when a short man with a congenial grin interrupted. "I used to be a farmer so I know all about growing food," he began, briefly lifting my spirits. "When I heard about this community garden thing I took a drive around town, to see what they looked like." He turned to me and shrugged. "They're ugly. No offense." Then back to the crowd: "But they are."

"We have a wonderful park already," a woman in a fashion tracksuit announced. "But *this*? This would turn it into a *hellhole*."

And so it went, each speaker explaining how awful a community garden would be for that site while the rest nodded and harrumphed in support. I fixed a smile on my face and settled in for a rout. Then a brown-skinned man entered in a wheelchair. At last, I thought, the reinforcements are here, and none too soon. I was wondering how to mention the fact that raised planting boxes would make growing food accessible for everyone, when it came his turn to speak.

"Thees plan ees terri-ble," he said. An Iranian couple behind him nodded vigorously in agreement. I kept my frozen smile as the next woman to speak called out from the side.

"Why we would need an *intercultural* garden anyway?" she asked as if it were some kind of disease.

I gestured to the table in front of me where someone (me) had dropped an issue of that day's free metro daily. The cover story was about violent attacks on gays and ethnic minorities. The headline read, "Vancouver #2 Hate City."

But they weren't interested in news. "You can't just waltz into our neighborhood out of the blue with this kind of thing," someone declared. It was the woman with jogging shoes. "Don't you even know you need to do a public consultation?"

I swept an arm to indicate me, her and the rest of the crowd, then held up my palms: wasn't this a public consultation? Unfortunately the gesture didn't include the city official who had organized the event and sat with me at the start of the deluge, but then had to leave for a more important meeting.

"We put up posters months ago," I explained. "We held five information sessions for people to learn more about it, including one right here in this community center. We had two larger town meetings for anyone interested to come talk about it and say how they'd like it go. Residents told us they were interested in having a community garden, and this was one of the possible sites."

More scoffing, more accusations of a plot to ruin their lives. I wondered how long a man could keep a smile on his face before pulling a muscle. A young couple arrived pushing a stroller. Great, I thought, now I can learn how many ways a carrot might harm a child. But they turned out to be all for it. The father, in a quiet voice, said, "Nobody uses that strip of grass anyway, do they? We could use it to help kids learn where their food comes from. You know what I mean?"

I did, but waited for someone else to say it. They turned instead to watch the entrance of a tall, tanned, white-haired man wearing a pinstriped suit worth more than my car. He explained, in lawyer-like fashion, why the proposal and the process itself were both flawed. When I didn't immediately agree, he explained it again. Then a third time. If I were on a jury, I thought, still smiling, I might rule against him just for being redundant, or maybe because of the suit.

The couple with the stroller slipped out, which was unfortunate because they would have had an ally in a short Asian woman who insisted on being heard even as others tried to interrupt. "I support this," she said looking from one blank face to another. "I think a community garden is a good idea." She had to raise her voice to get above the grumbling. "We *can* grow food in the city. Why not?

More healthy! Why should we have to get all our food from far away? We can grow ourselves. It's good for you! Good for the community! Something to do together!"

"You'll never get away with it," the woman in jogging shoes interrupted, looking at me. "Do you *know* how much I pay in property taxes? Where *do* you live anyway?"

I can't say I was surprised later when city staff, citing neighborhood opposition, turned down the proposal. I didn't take it personally. You win some, you lose some. But the neighbors' reactions still bothered me.

Was the idea of a community growing food together really so

Can't we and crops all just get along?   outrageous?

Was the sight of crops in an urban setting really that offensive?

If a modest proposal for a small food garden in an unused stretch of a park could generate that much heat, what hope did we have in our increasingly crowded cities for urban agriculture?

I took a little comfort in believing this crowd was not representative of the city as a whole. Someone told me they had also come out against a plan for an elementary school because — who knew? — it might attract youth.

But I also realized they weren't alone. Anyone proposing a food-growing project in the city can expect at least some opposition. More than a few people have made up their minds on this one. Farms may be fine, for out there, in the farmland where they belong, but here in the city we've managed to leave the muck and slop and smells behind. City people shouldn't have to endure the sight of their food until it's ready for them in the supermarket.

How did we get to this? How did we go in just a few generations from agrarian people with ties to the land and a respect for those who tend it to urbanites disgusted at the thought of anything even resembling a farm in our backyards?

Local man lost

I don't have *the* answer. But I have a start on a few answers that could add up to an explanation.

We are no longer grounded.

We have lost touch with our food and how it cycles through our lives from seed to plate to waste and back around.

We have swallowed the myth that small farms are inefficient and only factory farms can feed a hungry world.

We don't know how to grow our own food.

On that last point, you may think — so what? I also don't know how to build a lightbulb or plumb a home, but the lights and water still work, and when they don't I can call in an expert to help.

But the analogy doesn't account for the fact our lives are made poorer by our ecological ignorance. If we can't recognize the forces of nature moving around and through us, we can't live fully realized lives as a part of that nature. An unfortunate by-product of this modern disconnect is how we no longer understand the implications of our food.

We know little about how it was grown or raised, how it got to our plates or what happens to its remains when we're done. They could be feeding us poison and most people wouldn't even know it — but they should. Because it's wrong to live in mute submission to institutions powerful enough to keep us alive or drive us to an early grave. Here the Big Food corporations can (and will) be blamed, but they're only doing what they're expected to do, make a profit. The fact that we blindly buy into this makes us complicit. That the results are tragic for more than two billion people, and perhaps for the future of the Earth, should have us all looking at our collective shoes in chagrin.

But don't, not just yet. Keep reading instead. This book is not a pity party. We aren't here to weep and wail and gnash our teeth. It's fair to articulate the sorry state we're in, even to get angry about it, but I don't believe it's worth dwelling on the bad stuff, because things don't get done that way. Change is created by people who care, are committed to a cause and engaged in making things better. Such as farmers. The ones we need to help build the city of the future. The group you are being invited to join.

City on a thrill

The city I'm talking about is one with its food up front and the people who grow it an important part of the cultural community, rather than sad media stories or cartoon displays in corporate ads. In this city we will know the people who grow our food because they will be us.

Imagine a place shimmering under the canopy of the urban forest, the standard shade trees replaced by city orchards ripe with fruit and nuts. Picture the building walls green and alive with vine crops and vegetables in vertical gardens. See the berry shrubs defining the paths and decorating the park spaces. Watch locals of all ages, colors and backgrounds working together on the land, sharing tools, stories and harvests. Once-empty lots are now production-level farms. Flat roofs have come alive with crops and beehives. Aquaculture tanks with edible green covers are attractive features in public displays. Abandoned warehouses and factories have been reconfigured into indoor growing facilities for vegetables, fish, mushrooms and more. Organic fruit, flowers, herbs and vegetables taken fresh from the soil and still surging with vitality are sold citywide at farm gates, kiosks and street stalls.

Still with me? Or too much too soon? I realize that some people, benumbed by our present urban blight, may have difficulty conjuring up this scene. But it, or some version of it, is coming. By choice now or by necessity later. We will soon be a planet of nine billion people, with six billion living in cities. If the world is going to feed itself, cities must be transformed.

The city of the future will be a living, dynamic, holistic and edible place. The sooner we start growing it, together, from the ground up, the better it will be for all.

When I wrote *Guerrilla Gardening: A Manualfesto* (New Society, 2007), I thought everyone should see the city as a garden. Now I want everyone to see it as a farm. That's the aim of this book. It is written for:

- Urbanites seeking edible autonomy.
- Beginners intimidated by things like seed planting depths and compost carbon-nitrogen ratios.
- Gardeners who want to add food crops to their plant palates.
- Homeowners who would rather eat than mow their yards.
- Cubicle-bound dreamers who think tending the land may be more inspiring than working the copy machine.
- Entrepreneurs who count the number of urban consumers, the amount of unused urban land, and can do the math.
- Farmers who realize you can never learn enough about the amazing world of plants.

- Activists driving the new food politics on democratic, just and ecological grounds.
- Urban designers and planners using food and the ways it gets grown, processed, packaged, marketed, distributed, eaten and recycled to reshape our cities.
- Community developers tying health, environment, education, employment, transportation, waste recovery and more all together with urban agriculture.
- You, if you're none of the above but have still managed to read this far.

Reading plan

Inside this book you will find ideas big and small, designs of various examples, practical tips and words of experience from people with a few seasons on the farm under their belts. More than anything, it is hoped, you will find inspiration.

If you start at the beginning—where you are now—and read in a straight line, you'll take the most logical path to the end. The

Cuba figured out how to turn city lots into organic farms.

size of the growing operation goes up in scale with each chapter, for a while. We start out with a few plants in pots on a sunny kitchen windowsill. Then we move to the space of a typical apartment balcony using containers. Then to a backyard vegetable patch. We know we're getting serious when we dig up the whole backyard. Then there's no turning back, because we're after the front yard too. From there we move beyond residences to open spaces such as school yards and roofs that might better be turned into cropland. After that we ask what happened to the commons as we explore community gardens. We then make a pitch for their neglected cousin, community orchards. Next comes the rise of production-level urban operations, before we end with a glimpse into the future of city farms to see whether we really will end up with cows in high-rises.

That description may make things sound straightforward, but you can expect digressions amid blocks of general information that aren't necessarily bound by any particular scale. So chickens go in Chapter 4 about backyards, no problem there, but Soil 101 could have been added almost anywhere (it's in Chapter 3 where we start on backyard patches), and aquaponics could mean anything from a few edible aquarium fish and plants for your desktop to something grown at marketable level, as we shall see, but I have slotted it into Chapter 2 on container farms. Readers who prefer a meandering approach can always check chapter titles in the table of contents to get their bearings.

Because this book is written for a wide range of growers, from novices to pros, and makes no claims to inventing a new science or technology of raising food, you will probably find some of the information familiar enough to skim or skip. The ideas and designs offered here represent a collection of shared wisdom from a variety of sources, including my own experiences. If a notion resonates with you, try it in your own city, or first modify it to make it better and then try it. I'm guessing that most growers, typically both curious and ever keen to sweeten their luck with nature, will at least be interested in the prospect of hearing how others are doing these things. If nothing else, old hands might look at the section on how to dig a hole: turns out many of you are doing it all wrong.

The usual disclaimers

I feel bound to explain that although I've been lucky enough to earn my keep for the last five years in urban agriculture, I don't farm for a living. The fields I cultivate are in politics and the environment. I work through design, advocacy, community organizing and education. I don't grow crops for the market.

Most years, when I'm not too busy spouting to others, I grow food for myself and my family. I also help individuals and groups design, plant and manage food gardens, do consulting on urban greening issues including organic fruit tree growing, and work on municipal and regional policies to encourage more local agriculture. I've kept up with and even tried to encourage the trend toward scaling up into bigger spreads and larger yields because I'm convinced urban agriculture is necessary, and a growth industry. But as with many rural farmers these days, I don't have an easy answer to the hard question of how to make it pay.

I realize the threat to the family farm is not just a North American crisis. My involvement in local urban agriculture led me to a position on the board of directors of Heifer International, a nonprofit charity using the self-reliance model to help small farmers worldwide, including in North America. Situations are naturally different in each of the fifty countries where Heifer currently operates, but the strategies are based on a single idea: given the chance, communities will grow their own solutions to hunger, poverty and caring for the Earth.

That may sound simple enough to be true, but it is not a given. Most of our food now comes from places we don't know through a system run by corporations we don't recognize. We eat from a vast network run by Big Food—agribusinesses and chemical companies aided by financial speculators who hope to drive the small farmers of the world off their farms. Growing a monocrop over vast acres can be profitable, for a few, but not for the many (which is why the small farmer has to go) and not for the planet (we all pay the environmental costs for bills the big players never see). The crisis now facing the small farmer stems from being pitted in a rigged battle against factory-farm corporations backed by government support and subsidies.

What can be done? Plenty. Starting by going to the root of the matter, the way we grow our food. Every new urban farmer who enters the field is a soldier on our side, and every engaged urban consumer who buys consciously is an ally. If it seems like the odds are still stacked against us, maybe they are, for now. But hope is out there. Or rather, up there. The source of all life is still shining equally for all. No one can buy the Sun. Thanks to the miracle of our planet, the fact that plants eat sunshine, this earthly bounty is available to anyone. You still have to muster up the land (without necessarily owning it), as well as the gumption and some seeds

From soil to supper by way of a farmers' market.

and tools and things, but the magic is waiting for anyone determined to turn a seed into a meal and maybe even into a living.

This book is written with respect and gratitude for the urban agriculturalist. The city farmer. The town grower. The freethinking, hardworking visionary hero upon whom we will increasingly depend for our survival.

Long may you farm.

CHAPTER 1

HOME SWEET FARM
KITCHEN GARDENS IN THE KITCHEN

The new food revolution will be fought at home, meaning your home, in the kitchen. All the more reason to begin with the simple act of starting a few windowsill plants in pots, the nearest farm you'll ever know, which we'll discuss later in this chapter. But before we go there, let's agree on why this all matters and why the kitchen is the perfect place to start.

Big Food doesn't just want you off the family farm. It wants you out of the kitchen too, except for the minute or so it takes to zap some factory "fuud" product in the microwave—the polar opposite of a home-cooked meal using real food. Why? Because factory farming and factory fuud go together like high-fructose corn syrup and type 2 diabetes.

Let's forget for a moment the central role a traditional kitchen plays in the alchemy of spreading love through sharing food. Preparing a real meal takes time, which many of us now find in short supply. So is it really that wrong to pop a sixty-second solution into the microwave? If we're tired or busy and it's on sale and even says something like "healthy" or "lean" right on the package?

I won't judge, lest I be judged for the dubious food choices I make all the time, but I will point out that food is culture. When we eat, we ingest the physical world, accepting into our bodies the customs and values and politics of the system that got that food into our mouths.

For most of our history we have done this not as solitary beings but as members of a community. Only recently, with the spread of factory farms and the global food system, have we turned away from real food, local farm sources and meals as shared events. Nowadays we don't even think it strange to gulp down our calories standing over a kitchen sink or sitting behind the wheel of a car. And each time we do this, we lose a little of the culture that got us this far.

The French understand this point better than most, or are at least better able to articulate it. It was the French author and gastronome Jean Anthelme Brillat-Savarin who famously wrote, "Tell me what you eat, and I shall tell you what you are." But before we get too gaga over the French philosophy of food, you should know he also less famously wrote, "A dinner which ends without cheese is like a beautiful woman with only one eye."

Every culture treats eating as a unifying social ingredient, something important for more than calorie intake. The standard greeting in China is, "Have you eaten yet?" Just try to get out of a visit to an Iranian home without eating at least a few roasted seeds or baked sweets with your tea. You would struggle to name any popular festival or holiday anywhere in the world without its particular edible treats. Food is how we connect with our community, our planet and the best part of ourselves, the sharing bit.

At the same time, food has always been political. In the West we're just beginning to understand this, and connect the dots, recognizing existing links and creating others, using food policy to improve the rest of urban life. What excites activists these days is seeing how rapidly the idea spreads once people get it. We're at the stage now where the bandwagon is accepting passengers, and new entrants are climbing aboard in droves. Food policy as a concept contains multitudes, but it begins with where and how food is grown, which for city folks leads us back to urban agriculture.

Vancouver food systems educator Spring Gillard calls urban agriculture the "gateway" to understanding how food works (or doesn't) for a particular society. She leads workshops and lectures and writes on the topic for clients who include a growing number of urban planners and policymakers eager to understand how a society is defined by its food choices.

"It's the aspect of being more food self-reliant that people know the most," Gillard says. "And lately it's an absolute craze. I know several groups here running food gardening workshops that sell out constantly. The community gardens have two-year waiting lists. I think there's a lot of awareness around growing your own food, and a lot of people are going in that direction. If you can talk to people about growing your own food, talk about growing local, then you can start to expand to talk about local food and the other issues in the spectrum of food security."

Why you should be worried

That bandwagon metaphor was meant to be encouraging. Problem is, to stretch the metaphor even further, our bandwagon is stuck in a long traffic jam of SUVs. Urban agriculture crops represents a small portion of the global food market — 15 percent, according to the Food and Agriculture Organization of the United Nations (FAO). Although we may take some comfort in learning that there are 800 million urban farmers, and that the numbers are growing, it's still a daunting task to integrate city food into a global network that can serve for all.

If asked to name the biggest problem the world faces today, what would you say?

The energy crisis, perhaps. Our cities are built on a framework that may be about to collapse. The beginning of the end of the fossil fuel era is looming, or has already started, depending on which Peak Oil graph you believe. Quibble over the years left if you like, but you can't avoid the fact that in about a century we've burned up half the world's fossil fuels, which took billions of years to develop. And that was the easy half. The rest—costlier, dirtier and more dangerous to secure—could disappear much faster. Because the fundamental systems on which civilization has come to rely—manufacturing, transportation, agriculture—depend on a steady supply of affordable fossil fuels, you can see the potential for chaos.

Or you might say climate change. We're pumping enough pollutants into the atmosphere to alter global weather patterns. In other words, we're fouling our own nest. Droughts, melting ice caps and bigger weather disasters are all predicted and appearing in the daily news. Yet still we have no coherent global strategy to reverse the trend.

Both problems are ample cause for concern, but the more immediate response for at least one billion of your fellow passengers on the Earth would have been "hunger." In 2008 when prices of staple foods rose beyond the ability of the poorest to pay, riots broke out in more than twenty countries. Soldiers in the Philippines were called out to guard rice paddies and in Egypt the army was put to work baking bread.

Curiously, this happened during a time of record grain harvests and massive stockpiles. Later the role of Wall Street speculators was revealed in driving up the price of staples for profit. Certainly Big Food corporations reaped. Even as the United Nations declared "The Year of the Global Food Crisis," the *Wall Street Journal* reported food giant Cargill's profits rising 86 percent while pesticide and seed seller Monsanto doubled its earnings. If this all reads like a vague memory at best, it could be because 2008 later became better known as the year of the financial crisis. Huge banks and corporations seemed about to collapse under the weight of their own greed. You know already which crisis the world "leaders" swiftly agreed to solve.

What's food got to do with it? Agriculture is playing a huge role in using up what's left of our fossil fuels, and in trashing the planet. Carnivores, chew on this: according to the FAO, meat is responsible for 18 percent of the world's greenhouse gas emissions, which is more than for all transportation combined, including cars and planes. So your choice of meal on the flight may be more significant than the fact of flying. Chemical fertilizers? Made from ammonia derived from natural gas. Chemical pesticides? Petroleum-based.

You might think the environmental warning bells are ringing loudly enough to merit action, but the history of agriculture is not encouraging on this count. Famine, forced migration, wars, diseases and the collapse of civilizations can all be traced back to poor farming practices. Whenever a society loses its topsoil, its end is not far behind. But if you're wondering why those dunderheads in animal skins or togas weren't smart enough to take care of their own source of sustenance, don't be too quick to point historical fingers. As humans, it seems, we have yet to evolve to see the big picture. Maybe it's because we're hardwired to be tribal, good at protecting our own, for now, but not equipped to think collectively about how the wider society or our grandchildren are going to fare.

How bad is it? Already 90 percent of US cropland is losing its topsoil, and the worst of the losses are being reported in some of the richest farming areas. Iowa is losing topsoil 30 times faster than it is forming new soil. We may have already reached "peak soil."

An intergalactic observer evaluating the Earth would see at a glance that the industrial farm system is not working. It may successfully enrich the shareholders of a few transnational corporations, but its legacy is a billion hungry people and another billion confronting disease and early death from bad diets. And even if the factory farm system *did* work, and fed everybody with healthy food, it would still be a cause for concern given its dependence on a dwindling supply of fossil fuels. So although Big Food has given some of us the wonders of melons in January and the cheapest food in history, it is also killing us, slowly or quickly, and killing the only planet we have. Future generations might even view its reckless spending spree through our shared environmental resources as criminal.

If this all sounds bad, hang on; it gets worse. The solution from Big Food is to get bigger. Large corporations are gobbling up smaller corporations in a rush to control global market share, while still remaining curiously unknown. *The New York Times* editorialized on January 24, 2010, about "another behemoth lumbering towards consumers" in describing Big Food, but didn't mention four of the biggest by name. Cargill has been called "one of the world's most important companies," because it's all over your dinner table, but how many consumers have even heard of it? Or of its three competitors who make up the ABCD of Big Food: Archer Daniels Midland, Bunge and Louis Dreyfus?

In the 1960s the so-called "Green Revolution" described a plan to grow more food, particularly in poor countries, by planting new varieties of commodity crops on bigger farms with machines and chemicals. Like steroids in an Austrian weightlifter, the chemical strategy can work, for a while, if you measure success in limited terms such as muscle size. The long-term picture, however, may not be so pretty, either for the health of our 'roid-raging hunk or for agriculture.

The Green Revolution did indeed grow more food, while driving millions of small farmers off their farms. Many people who had been providing for their families using renewable practices that had succeeded for generations were turned into consumers unable to afford imported food.

As bad as the overall effects of this strategy were, they're trying it again, even borrowing from the tainted name. The Alliance for a Green Revolution in Africa (AGRA) may be counting on genetic engineering to create superplants to solve our food problems. You can imagine how giddy Big Food shareholders must be at the prospect of owning their own life-forms (which the US Supreme Court declared legal in 1980) and turning the world's farmers — who had saved their own seeds for millennia — into customers who have to buy new seeds from the company store every spring.

Why you shouldn't be worried

Whichever crisis you decided was the most critical — energy, climate chaos, hunger — urban agriculture offers a way to work toward the solution, starting now. Food is everything; our lives depend on it; it touches every aspect of the way we live. If we can solve the food issue, we can get to energy and health and the environment and poverty and more.

And that's where we come in. We know how to grow food. We've known it for thousands of years. It's within us. We may have gotten off track in the last century when we unwisely let industrial corporations take on the job, but now we're taking it back.

The good news is cities can save agriculture.

Yes, I know, this is usually put the other way around. Rural farms have fed urban areas for ten thousand years. But now it's

Cities and agriculture can (and must) save each other.

time to repay the favor. And cities are capable of doing it. The power of the urban consumer is multiplied by millions. A single good idea can sweep the country, and beyond.

If we manage to do this right by creating a fair and healthy food system that puts food choices back into local communities, regaining control over our bodies and the environment through "food democracy," it will begin with a new approach that includes urban agriculture. The way we shop and eat—and, of course, grow—has a powerful effect all the way down the food chain. Producers and consumers are already getting together on this through self-generated strategies such as farmers' markets that bypass the corporate system. If city folks can understand and embrace a network of farmers growing food that's good for people and for the planet, the tide will turn.

And when it does, city dwellers will start paying back a legacy of support to surrounding rural farms which will, after all, still be needed. Cities can grow a lot more food but not all of it. Nor will they need to if they're in a mutually supportive relationship with their adjacent countryside.

Rural communities in many parts of the world today are in dire circumstances, abandoned by young people as the corporate model sucks the life out of the family farm. Urban agriculture may help by inspiring innovations in rural farming, including environmentally friendly organic growing techniques. Cities might even supply the workers: traditional farmers are an aging group, so it's encouraging to see urban nonprofits, academic institutions and individuals training a new wave of young growers, some of whom will be happy to flee the concrete jungle to spread their wings.

Bean there, grown that

If it seems unlikely for urban areas to go from being gluttons to major providers of their own needs, consider that it has happened before. Farming was practised in some of the first known cities along the Tigris and Euphrates rivers four thousand years ago, and has been ever since, in varying degrees that sometimes reach impressive proportions. During World War II, city dwellers throughout North America dug up their lawns to plant victory gardens that supplied half or more of the vegetables eaten. "Our food is fighting!" read the poster for one American propaganda attempt to get more citizen-farmers behind the effort, and it worked: in 1943, twenty million food gardens were planted in the United States.

Urban agriculture is a part of our development as a species. It has always been and always will be with us. It's just that in times of crisis — like now, for instance — it ends up being even more with us.

In other words

To make sure we're all on the same page, let's agree on what we're talking about when we say "urban agriculture." Wikipedia, this week at least, calls it, "the practice of cultivating, processing and distributing food in, or around (peri-urban), a village, town or city."

That's a start, but it could be clearer, and avoid the clunky term "peri-urban." The Holland-based RUAF Foundation (Resource Centres on Urban Agriculture and Food Security) goes with a more user-friendly, "Urban agriculture can be defined shortly as the growing of plants and the raising of animals within and around cities." The RUAF website goes on to explain what this means:

"The most striking feature of urban agriculture, which distinguishes it from rural agriculture, is that it is integrated into the urban economic and ecological system: urban agriculture is embedded in — and interacting with — the urban ecosystem. Such linkages include the use of urban residents as labourers, use of typical urban resources (like organic waste as compost and urban wastewater for irrigation), direct links with urban consumers, direct impacts on urban ecology (positive and negative), being part of the urban food system, competing for land with other urban functions, being influenced by urban policies and plans, etc. Urban agriculture is not a relic of the past that will fade away (urban agriculture increases when the city grows) nor brought to the city by rural immigrants that will lose their rural habits over time. It is an integral part of the urban system."

Now we're getting somewhere. But even this expanded definition may fail to tell the whole story, because urban agriculture is in flux. This might turn out to be its most exciting time in history. All we can say for sure is that ten years from now it will not look like it does today. You like adventure? Start planting and strap in for the ride.

One size fits one only

City food growers can be divided into four main categories: home growers, community garden growers, institutional growers (schools, hospitals, companies, etc.) and market growers. Neat as this sounds, you can't count on it because the lines are being blurred. Home gardeners may get a taste and then search for empty lots to expand into. Commercial gardeners are growing in people's backyards. Some community gardeners raise funds selling honey and surplus crops. So who cares about the categories? The more city people growing city food, the better off we all are.

Styles of urban agriculture vary around the world. Even within North America the range is broad. Just as each city has its own arts scene and business culture and customs for driving, urban agriculture is absorbed by and influences the local culture. In Vancouver, the land is considered so developed a prospective site must be wrested from a battery of potential users, so community gardens get carved out a parcel at a time. But anyone from a crowded Asian megacity would see Vancouver as a wasteland of unused space.

The other end of the spectrum includes undervalued places like Detroit or Cleveland, where you can now buy a city lot, or lunch, depending on your mood. Some have even proposed a new homesteaders act for American cities to encourage growers to turn abandoned lots into urban farms. These could revitalize neighborhoods with jobs, greenery and local food. It won't be easy, but the original American dream, before it got corrupted into the current version of instant celebrity through reality TV, involved hard work on the land to reap the bounty of nature. Who's to say it can't happen again?

The word to know here is *usufruct*. We should make it part of our regular vocabulary. It means the right to use property (such as an empty city lot) that belongs to another (such as the city) provided you don't harm it. The notion comes from Roman law, the Latin terms *usus* and *fructus* equivalent to "use" and "fruits." Cuba offers usufruct land rights to anyone willing to farm empty city lots. Usufruct is also practiced in France as a way to use inherited property without outright owning it, and in Canada by some aboriginal nations which have usufruct rights to hunt and fish on public land. Pronounce *usufruct*, with caution, to rhyme with "lose a duct."

EIGHT REASONS TO START URBAN AGRICULTURE AT HOME

1. Eat healthier, live longer.
2. Not one of Michelin's 67 three-star restaurants around the world can produce a fresher salad than the one you just picked.
3. Home-grown tastes better. Who grows it, knows it.
4. An average-sized plot can save a family $500 a year.
5. Physical, mental, spiritual exercise.
6. Mow no more forever.
7. Food improves the local environment.
8. Urban farms enhance biodiversity, the web of life supporting us all.

A glance at the present state of the world's urban agriculture reveals widely different levels of progress. China is advanced—some two-thirds to three-quarters of the food people eat in the largest cities comes from farms in and around those cities. Practice helps: the Chinese have been living in and feeding themselves from cities for thousands of years. But even they can learn. I still shake my head in wonder at the tour group of city officials from near Shanghai who showed up in Vancouver to ask how we managed to blend food-growing operations with urban residents prone to complain about sights and smells. Welcome to the club, I commiserated, not sure how their interpreter would handle my advice to tell anyone who buys a new house in a known farming area and then complains about agriculture to "suck it up, buttercup."

Latin America is rapidly catching on. In Russia, some 70 per-

NINE REASONS TO START URBAN AGRICULTURE AS WORK

1. Options for involvement from part-time hobby to full-time investment.
2. Out-compete factory farms in quality and freshness.
3. Customers by the millions starting next door.
4. Micro-climates and the heat island effect can lengthen the growing season.
5. Small growing operations fit well in city nooks and pockets.
6. Clean, inspected water delivered to your site.
7. Urban farms contribute to and benefit from a strong local economy.
8. Crops soften the hard and artificial cityscape.
9. Create spin-off green jobs for you and your community.

cent of families are reported to grow at least some of their own food. African cities are more patchwork, but the rising popularity of urban agriculture is noticeable. Harare doubled its cultivation in just four years from 1990. In Somali refugee camps, people are being empowered to grow a new sense of community through raising food. Singapore has an estimated 10,000 urban farmers who produce 80 percent of the poultry and 25 percent of the vegetables eaten in the city.

Hot food

But mostly what cities have now is plenty of unplanted potential. One estimate says Londoners could grow up to 232,000 tons of fruits and vegetables, filling 18 percent of the city's nutritional needs. Massachusetts, which is largely urban and grows only 15 percent of its own food, could grow up to 35 percent, according to researchers.

We know growing food is hot right now in North America. Reversing a long-time trend, garden centers are now selling more vegetable seeds than flower seeds. The National Gardening Association reported a 19-percent increase in home food gardening from 2008 to 2009.

Reasons for the new popularity are many. Food scares in which people get sick or die are a popular media item. The trend toward city chickens received a boost in August 2010, when *half a billion* eggs were recalled from just two Iowa factory farms where salmonella had been detected. The declining taste of factory food has certainly had an effect on those whose memories still include real tomatoes. Others are motivated by concerns over industrial agriculture's role in land and water pollution, rural depopulation and the stripping of the Earth's thin topsoil. Any of these reasons could be enough to explain the popularity on their own; together they lead many people to wonder why anyone would choose *not* to grow at least some of their own food.

You're in

You may be wondering whether you're part of the club.

If you're growing food in or around a city, the answer is yes, you're an urban farmer. At least that's my take on it. Someone else may try to tell you otherwise.

Maybe you're not urban enough? If, like more than 80 percent of North Americans, you live in a place with paved roads and traffic lights and stores and nearby neighbors, it sounds to me like you're city.

The "farmer" designation may be another block for some. Doesn't that mean professionals? People who wear overalls to work? And earn their living raising food full time?

It could, but if profit were the chief criteria, where would we slot the farmers who have a bad year that puts them into debt? Or the ones who take an off-farm job to keep the operation going, or who have the sense to marry someone with money?

Some might suggest we should separate gardeners out from the real farmers because the real farmers are the ones who work at it full time. But then we might need a new category for all those

You grow, you're in: part of the crew from the Growing Power organization.

farmers who have to take on non-farm work or have the sense to marry spouses with jobs.

Another suggestion has been to reserve the title "farmer" for those who produce food for others. But would "others" not include the family members of someone growing vegetables to reduce the monthly food budget? What about someone who sells or trades or gives a portion of the harvest to friends, neighbors, the local food bank?

When I help community gardening organizations get growing, I often greet the members as "farmers." They smile at the title, but I'm being serious as well. I want them to feel included in a campaign that's bigger than any of us alone. I don't mean to dilute the significance of those traditionally dedicated to the art and science of providing our food. Rather the opposite. I believe widening the definition in this way opens the door to a greater sense of solidarity. A prime motivation for me in promoting urban agriculture is to get more people on our side—the independent growers and producers and packagers and recyclers (and, of course, eaters), who together will take back control of our food system. Starting with more independent growers. Because I believe the most profound way for people to discover the rich potential of local food is to get their hands into the soil, I say: welcome to the club, farmer.

Making the grade

By this point you may be encouraged, yet still curious to know whether you have what it takes be a farmer.

That's easy to answer. Anyone can grow or raise food, even (ahem) without a book. People have been learning on this job for thousands of years. You may have never planted a seed or pruned a tree, but you're still capable of becoming an urban farmer. There's a lot to learn, but that's part of the ongoing appeal. So if you're anxious, chill out. It isn't hard to grow things. Mother Nature is with you on this one. You just have to help. Give the plant or creature what it naturally wants and you'll get your food in return.

Don't worry if you think you may not have the right tempera-
ment for the task. Growers are like teachers or geologists or musi-
cians—they come in all kinds. One of the pleasures of researching
this book was the opportunity it gave me to meet more farmers
and learn about their daily lives. Naturally they're all different, but
as a group I do notice what I believe are some common characteristics. I find farmers in general to be savvy, stubborn, resourceful,
humble, patient, optimistic and generous—and maybe just a little
crazy to be doing this when the odds seem so stacked against
them.

A newcomer taking up this work today not just as a home-
grower but as a career farmer may seem just that—crazy—but
that's the spirit we'll need more of in the years to come. That's
why I'm in awe of anyone who can look at the global food system,
where even our governments have been sucked into subsidizing
corporate interests, and then look at the market, where returns
for small farmers have never been lower, and add a peek at the
weather, which is a dog's breakfast even in a good year, and still
say, "Screw it: I'm growing food anyway."

"History shows us that major changes are usually anticipated
by a few idealists, patient, persistent individuals who have been
following their personal convictions for many years before any
crisis arises," writes Joan Thirsk in *Alternative Agriculture: A History from the Black Death to the Present Day* (Oxford University
Press, 1997).

New urban farmers are a vanguard. If you can tap into that
collective energy and creativity and verve, you'll begin to believe
we really can rewrite the history books on food and reclaim agri-
culture from the grip of agri*business*. Every radish or carrot grown
and eaten in the city, with the help of sunshine and devotion, harvested when it's ready to eat rather than to meet some transport
schedule, is a victory for the community and the environment and
a beacon for the future.

Will it pay?

Urban farmers each have their own motivations, of course. For some it's to make money, although that doesn't seem to be the biggest attraction for most newcomers, at least at this stage in North America. Some do it because they believe farming has a crucial role to play in creating a better world. Some are into it because they're drawn to the magic of nurturing life that in turn supports other lives. Others do it because they know it's needed and they're just too ornery not to.

Urban farmers also come in all ages, genders, ethnic groups and backgrounds. Many are new to the activity, which is why it's so interesting. Cities are cultural mixes where ideas can cross-pollinate and thrive. Get artists and engineers and poets and dancers and plumbers and woodworkers and teachers working on the same problem and they'll all have something to bring to the mix that might not have happened back on the rural farm. This is good because if urban farmers are going to make a living, they'll need to consider new strategies in marketing and business that take advantage of the proximity and preferences of the customers nearby.

Mike Levenston was an early adopter before there was much of a concept to adopt. He began promoting urban agriculture in Vancouver in 1978, before, he says, there was a term for it. He founded and still runs the informative and fun City Farmer website, the go-to place for urban agriculture news from around the

One more carrot for the cause.

world. Levenston also manages a demonstration organic garden used to teach city folks how to practise urban farming and composting. He has seen the trends in city food ebb and flow over the decades. He takes encouragement from all those coming into it, but reminds them how it's really all part of the same-old.

"People who never thought they would be interested in growing food—because that was something left to the farmers—are now growing food. Planners are getting into it, corporations are getting into it. In the last five years, there's been a shift toward more people trying to make a living with urban agriculture. This is a brave new world and it's going to be very interesting to see where and how that goes.

"On the other hand, I like to point out to people who rave about how new this all is that we have had Chinese market gardens next to Vancouver in Burnaby since the 1800s. These guys are not in the news because they're not in the same political camp—they aren't organic, they're not the new economic types, they're not blowing any horns as part of the new urban agriculture. But it is urban agriculture to the tooth, and it's working for them."

Levenston's conclusion on the economic viability of urban agriculture today: "I'm not the one to ask because I got into it from the environmental side—getting people to tear up their lawns—rather than the commercial side. But I would say this: it's probably good to have a spouse helping you somehow. If you want money, go get a regular job."

Sprout up

If you're going to start small, you can't get much smaller than the wee but powerful sprout.

Why bother? Because you can enjoy fresh, tasty, homegrown greens all year long without leaving the kitchen—if your kitchen has a windowsill that gets at least some light. For those lacking even a single sunny window, welcome to Vancouver, and we'll look at other lighting options toward the end of the chapter.

Yes, I'm talking about sprouts, those little powerhouses of enzymes and nutrients that can turn a boring sandwich or salad into a lunch with zing. Don't skip ahead on us here because you've already been there/done that between making macramé pot-hangers and tie-dyeing T-shirts. There is more to the world of sprouts than alfalfa.

You also needn't shy away because you're concerned about poisoning yourself with *E. coli* or something else scary you may have seen in the news. It's true that there have been cases where sprouts have gone bad and people have gotten sick; a few have even died. Sprouts aficionados tell us the products in question came from large factory-sized operations, not homegrowers. Of course, you will need to practise good hygiene. But as long as you start with clean seed, your chances of food poisoning are probably higher if you eat manufactured foods sourced outside your home rather than something you grow yourself from seed.

The proof is in the pudding. Sprouts are wispy but pack a nutritional punch far above their weight class. To quote Bob Rust from

NINE REASONS TO START A SPROUT FARM

1. Minimal investment required.
2. Tiny plants don't need acreage or tractors.
3. Harvest is easy with scissors.
4. Short growing period minimizes impact of a single botched batch.
5. Revenue possible in weeks rather than months.
6. Can skip a batch to take a break without losing the season.
7. Can farm year-round indoors.
8. Market is underdeveloped and competitors are few.

the website of the International Sprout Grower's Association, "Most of the phytochemicals found in vegetables originate in the seed." These phytochemicals, which may be able to prevent diseases including cancer, "are not any higher in a mature vegetable than in the seed from which it came." Rust says there are approximately a thousand plants per ounce of cabbage sprouts, and each one is a nutritional wonder. "You would need to eat many ounces of mature cabbage to consume one plant. This is why an ounce of sprouts can be a thousand times as potent in some phytochemicals as an ounce of the mature plant."

Whether any of that is true, or whether you want to eat a thousand heads of cabbage, I can't say. I can declare that sprouts are a beautiful crop to watch grow. It may take you back to memories of grade one when you first planted a pea in a cup and came back each day astonished to see how much it had grown. The marvel of plants in progress is constant with sprouts, and the aesthetics will brighten any kitchen window or plate they end up on. Sprouts come in a variety of colors, from lime green to yellow to purple, and they all look good mixed in a salad.

Name that green

The nicely written and gorgeously photographed book *Microgreens: A Guide to Growing Nutrient-Packed Greens* by Eric Franks and Jasmine Richardson (Gibbs Smith, 2009) ranks the various tiny plants by their stages of development.

Sprouts are what you get in the first stage of germination. Grown in warm and moist conditions, they are harvested just after they germinate. They tend to have a pleasantly crunchy texture.

If sprouts are left to grow a little longer — typically in soil, although other media can work too — they will develop their first leaves, known as cotyledons. At this stage they can be harvested as microgreens, which the authors are all over. Because they absorb some of the micronutrients from the soil, microgreens are even more nutritious than sprouts. They are tender and flavorful, looking and tasting more like a salad green than a "wiry" sprout. (No hint of bias here on the part of the authors.)

Following the cotyledons, plants will put out their first "true" leaves, which grow into the recognizable leaves of the crop itself. In a week or two they will reach the cute "baby green" stage popular with fine restaurants and refined customers who understand, as the Japanese do, that a meal is first consumed with the eyes.

No, you taste it

There is a risk in growing sprouts. The conditions you provide for the seeds to germinate are also ideal for pathogens. These pathogens may be present on the seed before you even get started, grow with your sprouts, then cause food poisoning when eaten. The worst recent case involved radish sprouts served in school lunches in Sakai City, Japan, in July, 1996. The sprouts, contaminated with *E. coli*, caused three deaths and nine thousand illnesses, mainly diarrhea. As nothing was found at the hydroponic growing facility, the source was believed to be the seeds. The government issued a hygiene practice manual for radish sprouts later that year and no major outbreaks have been reported in Japan since.

Bound by concerns for safety and liability, governments tend to be wary of home-sprouting operations, although they stop short of telling growers not to try. Instead they point out how salmonella or, less frequently, *E. coli* contaminations have afflicted people eating raw sprouts around the world. Health Canada, for example, advises Canadians that raw or undercooked sprouts should *not* be eaten by children, older adults, pregnant women or those with weakened immune systems. A UC Davis Department of Agriculture and Natural Resources study recommends buying certified pathogen-free sprout seeds only and then heating them on a stovetop for five minutes in a solution of 3-percent hydrogen peroxide. However, that would seem overly protective to most home and small-scale sprout farmers who have grown successfully and safely for many years.

Rinse and repeat

Growing instructions for the various types of sprouts are readily available online or at the library or bookstore. For a container, the Primal Seeds (primalseeds.org) site suggests the good old standby jar, which is simple and easy to procure but may not be the best choice because it tends to cram the sprouts into the middle. Other options include a tray with drainage holes smaller than the seeds, or bags such as those made out of linen or hemp, which can be rinsed together with the seeds and then hung up to dry.

For most types of sprouts, seeds are first soaked for 12 to 24 hours. Drain and rinse the seeds once or twice during soaking. Then spread the soaked seeds out in your jar, tray or bag. Some, such as alfalfa, do not need light, so your sprout farm can be a closet (in a few days when the sprouts have reached their full size you can put them in the light for a few hours to green up).

Rinse your growing sprouts at least every 12 hours, more frequently in hot weather. Make sure the container drains well since standing water invites rot. If you are using a simple jar with a cheesecloth-held-by-elastic cover for rinsing, tilt the jar with the open mouth down onto a plate so any excess water can run out.

You'll see when the sprouts are ready because they'll reach the size you want and start looking scrumptious. Harvest by cutting with scissors and then store the sprouts in a plastic bag in the vegetable crisper of the fridge, where they should keep for a week or so. Discard any that turn brown or smell odd.

What to sprout? The selections are as varied as you'll find on a vegetable farm. Alfalfa is the standard you remember from your granola days, and still popular for good reason: it means "father of all foods" in Arabic. Radish and mustard offer tangy or, with a little more time, hot additions to a mixed green salad. Buckwheat and sunflower grow into bigger, more robust sprouts that can work in salads and stir-frys. You'll recognize the familiar mung from Chinese cooking. Wheat can be used to bake sprouted grain bread. Barley and peas can all be sprouted and then cooked by steaming or sautéing. Lentils are a slightly spicy favorite. Oats have a mildly milky flavor, but can be difficult to separate from the hull. Garbanzos sprout easily but also go bad easily; more reliable is the miniature kala channa version, if you happen to be near an East Indian food store.

Sprout farmer — Chris Thoreau

For tips on taking a sprout farm out of the kitchen and into bigger production, I asked a professional, Chris Thoreau.

A student in agroecology at the University of British Columbia, Thoreau wanted a summer job that would let him grow food and make money at the same time. We met at his sprout farm, a 40-foot-long covered bench on a flat grassy area in an industrial zone behind a factory producing salad dressing and mayonnaise; the "opposite end of the food chain," he noted wryly.

Why sprouts?

"Nobody's growing spouts. If you're going to do the farmers' market you need a niche product. Also this is 2,000 square feet.

Chris Thoreau.

My return per square foot is way beyond what anybody can do on a farm. The bench space is 200 square feet. I could compress this down to a backyard. You can't grow $24,000 worth of beets in your backyard. So if I want to make an income in the city I needed a model that can do that and this was it."

Thoreau built his sprout farm by erecting a row of covered growing tables out of two-by-fours and chloroplast, or corrugated plastic. He installed an irrigation line, a cleaning/packing table, and *voilà*, he was off and growing.

"I want this to be a duplicable model. The beauty of it is you can do it anywhere. You can do it in a parking lot, you can do it in a driveway, you can do it on a rooftop. All you need to do is build a bench. That's what makes it a good urban model."

Thoreau is growing sunflower sprouts that can serve as a salad green or sandwich filler. They come from black sunflower seeds, the variety typically used for oil production or birdseed. He feels he got a good price, 500 pounds of seeds for about $2,000. There are cheaper seeds, but he wanted these for the quality. You can also pay more, but he found a distributor with older seeds, which haven't been a problem since they still germinate at a 90-percent rate. The resulting sprouts are tasty enough to attract buyers at $5 for a medium-size freezer bag (180 grams). As a former certified organic inspector who also has experience running a small organic farm, Thoreau is still searching for a good source of organic seed.

Sunflowers work well, he said, because they have so much energy embodied in the seed. By the time he harvests, they haven't taken anything out of the soil, so he doesn't even need to replenish the nutrients. Radishes, he's found, extract more, so before he diversifies into other crops he's going to research the best growing mixes.

Growing sprouts for market looks easy, and he tells people it is, but he admits he doesn't tell them everything. Even with something like sprouts on a bench, the beauty of growing food is that you're never sure what nature will provide until you try it, so the learning process is unending.

"The trick is growing them to get that nutty flavor. If they grow too fast you don't get it. If they grow too slow, well, you do get it but you don't get a very big sprout. I sell by weight so I want the biggest sprout I can get without compromising the integrity of its flavor."

Thoreau is keen to emphasize the entrepreneurial potential to growing food. "Most urban farmers are probably not making money. They're doing it as a hobby, as a love. But I want this to be my living. So I wanted to develop a model that can pay for itself as well. Last year was pretty good. I was in the black. On average I made about $2.50 an hour, which is probably about par for farming. And then I did a business plan and went from there."

Still cringing at the math, I had to interrupt for a clarification.

"Yes, $2.50 an hour, after paying off expenses. When I was telling my accountant he was like, 'You know you're actually expected to lose money at the beginning, right?'"

Thoreau looks at the three components of sustainability — environmental, social and economic — and figures he has them covered. He knows how to grow environmentally from his experience on organic farms, and he's aware of the need to conserve water. Economically, he wants to make money. But socially, he knows it's not just about the money. His idea of a sustainable enterprise is not one that forces him to work 70-hour weeks. So he puts in an average 31 hours per week. That includes selling at two farmers' markets and to a few restaurants and grocery stores. With sprouts, he has to guess what the market will want in ten days when his seedlings are ready to eat, because he can't just wait an extra week like a farmer with beets in the ground. Although he does have some leeway in timing thanks to five coolers that can each hold sixty bags of sprouts until market time.

We were talking in September when there were still a few weeks left in his growing season. I wondered whether he had any idea so far whether it would work out to be a profitable year.

"Oh yeah, I know in real time. I record every hour I do, every penny I spend, every bag I sell. I have to because otherwise I won't know whether this is viable or not. You can wing it, and I kind of winged it last year, but still I applied the numbers. Basically if I'm only making $2 an hour like last year then I have to look for something else to pay my rent. Right now I'm at $7.50 an hour, but I have no major expenses left. I buy all my seeds at the beginning of the year, all my bags, all my sanitizer, my compost, everything. I've got enough compost and seed to last me into next year. So I'm

Walk This Way

Examples & Inspiration

The Urban Farming group started in Detroit in 2005 with a straightforward plan to create food gardens where people needed them most. From the three launched that year, the group has expanded into thirty cities across the US with the equivalent of more than eight hundred gardens based on its twenty foot by twenty foot model. The group says "our harvest is free for everyone to enjoy" and encourages neighbors to share their food with local food banks to help others in need. Key programs include Community and Green Science Gardens, Urban Farming Food Chain, Edible Walls and Rooftops, Health and Wellness, Environmental Justice and Green Collar Jobs.
— urbanfarming.org —

in the black and I'll stay in the black because I've already covered my expenses. I have a bit of labor to spend. But I'm still not in the black to not do any other work at all. I do some other stuff, but this is my main source of income."

I wondered if he could double his scale, maybe grow enough to get his return up to say $14 an hour? And then, who knows, double it again?

"The one thing that most urban farmers probably don't have is a business plan. I made a five-year plan this year. I've doubled production from last year. Last year I did about $11,000 in sales. This year the goal is $22,000. I don't think I'll actually reach that but I'll be just under. My costs are 50 percent. So to get that will cost me $11,000."

Not a huge payoff, but then he is doing something he wants to do.

"Exactly. And that'll go up in the future. In retrospect I spent a lot of money this year I didn't need to spend. Some of that is other expenses. Like I had to replace the drive train on my bike—I do 95 percent of my deliveries by bike. So I'm generally at about 50 percent. I'd like to be at 40 percent."

I wondered whether sprouts are as easy as they look to grow.

"They are. I think sprouting is probably the most untapped urban agriculture resource. We're so fixed on sustenance from calories we forget about nutrients. And a tray of these is probably your vitamins for a week. The same thing, you can do your alfalfa in a jar. I talk a lot about sprouts. I tell everybody how to do this at home. This is how I do it; this is how you could do it. There are a lot of little things I don't tell them so they'd have a hard time pulling it off, but people don't have time anyway. But it is easy. The key is you have to rinse them a lot during the day to keep them fresh. In the hot weather I used to rinse five times a day, and that's what you need to get a good sprout. People aren't going to do that. If they're gone at eight in the morning and back at six for their job, it won't happen."

He advises young farmers to start with a business plan.

"I don't know why more people don't do them. I look at how the history of this evolves. Urban agriculture is how agriculture started, in a sense. In the '80s and '90s urban agriculture was a fringe thing — people growing food in weird places or tearing up their lawns or driveways. It was kind of an alternative movement. Now it's shifting. Like, I'm an entrepreneur, and I think that's where it needs to go. That's why I focus on the economic side of it. If it can generate income, it's more sustainable. If you think about all the nonprofit groups you work with, you're always struggling to find money, worried about how you're going to function. Well, one way is to generate income yourself. So that economic sustainability is a key part of urban agriculture moving forward. We have to look at this as a way to make a living."

Space invaders

Indoor growing systems are plentiful these days, with a lot of companies emerging to take advantage of the home food-growing trend.

The designs tend to blend futuristic with fun. Such as GAMA-GO's Power Planter, modeled after a nuclear power plant, only instead of radiation leaks you get wheat grass sprouts emerging from the ventilation stack. Or there's the Grobal from designer Karim Rashid and the Vitamin Living pot with a drip-rate-adjustable IV bag drip hanging above your plant as if it were an ailing patient. Think of these planters as the lava lamps of the 2010s. Kind of funny, the first time, with the bonus of providing something to eat too. A selection of these and some more whimsical indoor plant options can be found on Heavy Petal's garden-related website (heavypetal.ca).

Window farming is a way to grow up to 25 plants in the space of a typical 4' × 6' window. You get a spiffy visual upgrade for your home, lots of backlit vibrant green amid a "lush, trickling, fountain-like curtain," and, of course, you get food. Lettuce, spinach, basil, cherry tomatoes, beans—whatever you like to eat, you can grow in a window thanks to a hydroponic flow system that provides the plants' nutrient needs.

The Window Farming website (windowfarms.org) also has kits for sale. The smallest, holding sixteen plants in eight containers, takes an estimated two hours to set up and sells for $149.95. Check availability for your area—as of the winter of 2010 they weren't shipping beyond the US.

You can also create a version of the window farm on your own—admirably, the website encourages it. The possibilities are limitless, with tinkering and geekdom rewarded. From the same site you can click to our.windowfarms.org/tag/officialhow-tos/ for personal accounts and tip-trading from "an open source community developing hydroponic edible gardens for urban windows."

You ought to be able to find the materials you need for a window farm on a short shopping trip around town. A small pump (with enough power to lift water from the bottom reservoir to the top of your window), 6-mm tubing, plastic (or your preferred material) bottles and clay pellets to grow in should all be available at the hardware, garden or pet store (if it includes aquariums).

I've grown a sort of window farm before—the hot chilies seemed to appreciate the extra heat through the window—but not hydroponically like these ones. It strikes me that these kits—or homemade versions of them—would appeal most to tinkering types, the kind of people who love to experiment for its own sake. They look like they would be fun to build and operate.

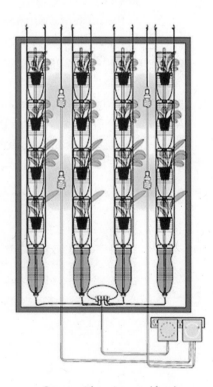

Room with a view *and* food.

Elaborate window farms may even be comparable to some pets: worth the fuss for those who own them, but more trouble than they're worth in the eyes of outsiders. If you do get started, though, you get to farm right where you are, in all kinds of weather, while enhancing your interior design at the same time. Some people might even consider fiddling with the minor technology involved in the contraption a plus.

What if you don't even have a window? (I ask this abjectly while staring out my home office at the construction scaffolding and work crew in their sixth month of repairing my leaky co-op). You might consider something like the "fool-proof, dirt-free, indoor garden device" known as the Aerogarden. I admit I was tempted. This is another hydroponic appliance, but it comes with its own timed lighting system so you don't even need window space. The device tells you when to add water and nutrients, everything done at the push of a button. It looks pretty nifty in the pictures, a little like a Star Trek prop, but I wondered how clean and galactic it would look after a few months of growing. Also holding me back was the cost; the elite model I wanted was selling for $200, which would make every bean it grew awfully dear. Then again, people pay more than that for interior decorations I think are useless and you can't eat a thing from, so maybe it's still a good idea.

TAKE HOME MESSAGE

There's no farm like home.

CHAPTER 2

CONDO ACRES
CONTAINER FARMING
FOR CONFINED SPACES

More people might become urban farmers if they had urban farms. What's an apartment-dweller with nothing but a narrow balcony in the sky to do?

Plant it. If the sun is shining on your space, you're in a farmable area. Even if it isn't, if you can see blue sky, you still have options.

Vegetables, edible flowers, cooking herbs, berry shrubs and fruit trees are all beautiful and nutritious, but they're also kind of dumb. They don't know if they're in a pot. They may have evolved over thousands of years to grow in the ground, but that doesn't make it the only place they will grow. Give your plants the basics they need and they will sprout and develop and flower and fruit even hundreds of feet in the air on a balcony or on a crowded ground floor patio outside your doorstep.

The secret to a successful container farm is to think like a plant. Just figure out what a plant needs, then provide it.

You can make this approach simple or complex. The complex part has its charms, in that you can spend a lifetime on horticultural experiments conducted in those fascinating mini-laboratories we call pots. But let's stick with the simple here because, really, it's all we need to grow food.

So what does a plant need?

Sun. Water. Nutrients. Space.

Before we discuss each one, here's a primer in how the magic all starts, with the planting of a seed.

How to plant a seed

Poke a shallow hole in the soil with your finger, drop the seed in, cover it with more soil and add water. Now relax; you're done.

That's pretty much all there is to it. If you've never tried before, because you were worried about getting the technique just right, you now know enough to grow trainloads of food.

Much of my work in teaching newcomers to grow into urban farmers involves leading them by the hand past this first step.

TEN REASONS TO START A BALCONY FARM

1. Proximity encourages participation.
2. Reduce food miles to footsteps.
3. Harvest year-round using covers, lights, insulation.
4. Growing space is expandable with stakes, trellises, overhangs.
5. Crops improve the view from inside.
6. That grimy barbecue? Hide it with food plants.
7. You're also making an eco-friendly habitat for birds and bugs.
8. Balconies have fewer weeds to manage than in-ground farms.
9. No worries about contaminated soils.
10. Protected warm areas can extend types of plants possible.

Some beginners are intimidated by what they think will be difficult, something that needs expertise and the green-thumbed experience of a long-time grower or professional farmer. The truth is, I tell them, anyone can, and everyone should, grow food because all you're really doing is providing the conditions nature wants to do the real work. The seed knows what to do.

But that doesn't quite fill a workshop, so I go on to provide some details. The proper planting depth and spacing for the seeds? That's usually easy—they're written right on the package. But I've yet to see a grower take out a ruler to determine whether the seed is ½-inch or ¾-inch deep. Close enough works. A rule of thumb if you don't like reading instructions or were given the seeds with no package details is to plant them 3–4 times as deep as their width. So a tiny carrot seed goes just under the surface, while a pea would go a fair bit below that.

Space case

Seed spacing recommendations are also typically written on the package, but are ultimately up to the planter. Picture your mature radish or beet or zucchini plant to get an idea of how far apart you should plant the seeds. Growers often overseed to make sure they get crops even if the germination rate is less than 100 percent, or because they find way too many seeds in the package and don't know what else to do with them (buying collectively with fellow farmers can help solve this problem).

This usually means they have to thin the new seedlings out later, leaving only the biggest and most promising plants with plenty of room to develop. But many beginners turn out to be bad at thinning. It can be tedious, but I think this has more to do with the fact that they're thrilled to have created a grand display of edible vitality, and killing most of it just seems wrong. Nevertheless, you must cull those extras. If you don't, you may be left with a thick, crowded row of, say, carrot tops that never manage to develop into carrots.

So when it comes time to thin, don't dwell on the seedlings you're taking out. Focus instead on the ones you're keeping, then simply remove the rest nearby that threaten your prizes. You can just yank out the unwanted growth, but if the roots are already growing together it's safer and easier to snip the stems off near the base with scissors. And you will often get a tasty fresh salad from the sprouts and microgreens you thin.

Back to the seeds you just planted: cover them with some of the surrounding soil and press down lightly with your palm or foot to eliminate large air pockets. Germination doesn't start until the seed comes into contact with moist soil.

Now begins the most critical stage of the growing process. Once germination starts, you must keep the soil irrigated until the plant is established. If the soil dries out and the wisp of a root has no moisture to absorb, the plant will dry up and die. In containers, especially on a hot day, this can happen sooner than you might think, so keep a close eye out to make sure your babies stay well watered.

To extend the growing season, seeds can be started indoors and then transplanted outside once the weather permits. Tomatoes are a favorite choice for this in Canada, because you get to begin your farming activity as early as February, a worthy indoor pursuit to take your mind off winter. Remember to toughen up your seedlings in spring by placing them outdoors in a protected area for a few days before you transplant them. Plants don't like to be shocked by cold any more than people do.

Here comes the Sun

Plants need sun because that's what they eat, sunlight. The name for this, which you learned in school, is photosynthesis, and it is an amazing thing. You can thank photosynthesis for the fact that you are alive, and the Earth is a living planet, and gorgeous to boot. If plants did not have chlorophyll that captures energy from the Sun and converts it into sugars which fuel plant growth, we might be a planet of fungi.

Learn to think of leaves as solar panels. Observe the fascinating range of shapes and sizes and textures they present. Appreciate the architecture of each plant as it marshals its forces into a strategic arms race with all the other plants, each working out its own balance between rapid growth and sturdy stems to get its solar collectors into the light.

Your duty is to provide the opportunity for your plants to reach that light. Vegetables, we are told by all the gardening books, need at least six hours of sun per day.

Well, yes and no. Most vegetables do indeed prosper under full sun. If you were going into food growing as a business, you would not choose a shady location. However, many urban residents lack the luxury of picking their home farmland. A lot of urban balconies are on the wrong sides of buildings or partially shaded by other buildings so they get less than the guidebook-mandated six hours.

We're all sun worshippers when it comes to growing food.

Don't give up. There are vegetables that can get by with just four hours of direct sunlight. This will be comforting news to some, but what if you don't even get that much on your tiny outdoor homestead in the sky?

You still shouldn't give up. Even the four-hour requirement can be fudged.

One way is to choose vegetables that will reach maturity or an edible stage without needing a lot of sunlight. Think of leafy greens such as lettuce, spinach, kale and chard. They do everything in a single stage. Rooting crops (beets, turnips, onions) must grow leaves as well as large root sections, which is more energy-intensive. Fruit-bearing vegetables (tomatoes, cucumbers, eggplant) need the most sunlight of all, first to put out the leaves and roots, then to produce the flowers and fruit needed for a harvest.

If you're reading this in the northern hemisphere on your north-facing balcony and are now despondent, hold on. You still aren't allowed to give up. There's always a chance to grow something. One summer for an experiment I tried growing broccoli in a container on a ground-floor balcony facing south, but mostly covered overhead by an eave and facing a two-story-tall purple-leaf plum tree. I didn't do precise calculations but I supposed it was getting about two hours of sunlight in the morning. The rest of the day it sat in shade.

And it did just fine. For testing purposes I planted the same type of broccoli in a sunny spot in the ground. The ground broccoli grew faster and bigger, but several weeks after I ate it, I was able to cut a sizeable head from my shade-bound balcony experiment, and it was delicious. The mini-heads that emerged in the following weeks were good for a few more meals, and the leaves weren't bad at all in a soup.

I was of course happily surprised, having expected the experiment to fail. Why did I get these good results? I believe it has something to do with the nature of sunlight. We often read about how many hours of direct sun a growing plant needs. Whether it gets it isn't hard to see if you follow the arc of the sun across the sky. But this doesn't take into account the reflected, or maybe that's refracted, light. We get a lot of this in Vancouver. Many days a high cloud cover will paint the sky gray. We call it a cloudy day, but there's still plenty of light coming through. It isn't coming from one obvious source, but rather from all directions above. The plants capture this light and use it to do what they do best.

So if you can see the sky from where you stand on your balcony, your space has at least the potential to capture light. And maybe that's enough to try your own experiment.

Here's another trick to capture as much light as possible: plant your prizes into wheeled containers that can be moved throughout the day to capture sunlight as it shifts. This strategy is time-intensive and maybe a little too obsessive for most, but I've learned to never underestimate the enthusiasm of a grower determined to get the world's tastiest tomato.

Water, water, everywhere

Your plants need water, constantly. To dry up completely is to die. We have already described why the seedling stage is so critical. Like a baby, these tiny and adorable little creatures are helpless on their own. Later, when the plant is bigger and its root system more extensive, it will be able to go longer between watering times. Roots and stems and leaves can all hold water, but not for long, so you must make sure that your balcony plants are properly irrigated. The water-holding capacity of your soil will obviously be limited by the size of your container.

Dealing with this is becoming easier with more options in containers. Now you can buy "self-watering" pots. With that description you might expect them to march to the tap and turn it on, but it actually means they have bottom sections that can be filled with water. Roots tap into the reservoir to lift moisture up to the rest of the plant. Such pots can cut your watering chores from every day to once or twice a week, depending on local conditions.

Slow food meet slow water.

They're handy to have if you're less than diligent or know you'll be away for a few days.

You can also buy water-retention gels to add to your growing mix. Starch-based hydrogels are supposed to absorb a hundred times their weight in water and then slowly release it into soil—but I've never tried them to find out whether that number makes any sense. You can also try using a bottle filled with water, then turned upside down and stuck into the soil so the contents slowly drain out. A nicely designed and colored bottle may look less trashy than a plastic pop bottle, although the latter may help make a statement about recycling—knowing as you do now that Americans buy an estimated 29.8 *billion* water bottles every year. I'm not a statistician but I believe that adds up to enough plastic for every American to bury a small country of his or her choice. Another way to help keep water in a container longer is to use mulch on the surface. Compost, straw, grass clippings, bark chips and moss can all help slow the process of your soil drying out.

Feed your head of cabbage

I said your plants eat sunshine, which was true, but they also need a few essential nutrients to keep the process going. These nutrients are taken up by the plants and removed by you when you harvest, or are flushed out with watering, so you must regularly replenish your soil. Organic fertilizers are the preferred choice (more on why later). You can add these as a liquid fertilizer in small amounts each time you water, every two weeks during the growing season, or in bulk when you create your growing mix to start a new container.

Organic growers are pleasantly surprised to find more varieties of fertilizers available in the garden stores every year. This is happening only because more customers are asking for them, so if your garden store is lagging on the selections, let them know. If they get old-school testy and tell you synthetic fertilizers are just as good or better, don't argue about all the fossil fuels and greenhouse gases involved in making the artificial stuff. Just ask if they know the address of another garden store nearby that carries organic products.

Media frenzy

The easiest way to fill your balcony pots is to buy bags of potting soil, preferably organic, at your local garden store. They're easy to carry and do a good job of keeping the soil contained until it's ready to be emptied into the containers. But you can save money and gain some control over this crucial aspect of your container farm by mixing your own.

Remember, we want to think like a plant. What does a plant need in a mix for its growing medium? Something that can provide support for its roots, hold water and oxygen, and deliver nutrients. The possible combinations are many. They can even include soil-less mixes: notice the list of needs doesn't specify that they be met by soil.

But topsoil is relatively cheap and easy to get, so you're probably better off starting with it before you get into more esoteric materials. The easiest and cheapest way to get some would be to walk into a garden with a shovel and fill your container with garden soil. But you will not do this because you know garden soil contains too much clay, which would dry and harden into a cement-like block your plants would hate.

Here's a combination that works well: two parts sifted compost or potting soil, one part vermiculite or perlite (neutral minerals

that have been heated until they expand into popcorn-like particles to help absorb water or improve drainage) and one part
organic fertilizer. Some people recommend peat moss in place of
the vermiculite or perlite because it works like a sponge to absorb
and hold water. But others scold the peat-moss-raiders because
it took something like ten thousand years to grow every inch and
now it's being overharvested. These types suggest instead using
coir, or coconut fiber, which absorbs well and is so plentiful on the
planet it was considered garbage in countries like Sri Lanka until
they realized how much Western growers would pay for it.

If you're not sure which to choose between perlite or vermiculite, feel free to spend a few hours on the internet following the
debate. Briefly, vermiculite is made from a silica-like mineral
and mined in places such as South Africa, China and Brazil. Its
orangey-brown color tends to blend with the dark brown of the
rest of your planting mix. Perlite, a volcanic material, is as white as
popcorn and may float and settle at the top when your container
is flooded.

Some growers combine the two as they have complementary
properties: vermiculite helps to hold water, which is important
for containers, while perlite helps to drain water, which is also
important for containers. Others skip the vermiculite because if
you include too much and it absorbs a lot of water it can make the
whole mix kind of mushy. A few are wary after reading how it was
reportedly contaminated with asbestos in a mine in Libby, Montana, in a way that led to hundreds of illnesses and some fatalities.
I don't believe vermiculite from mines in other places is similarly
asbestos-contaminated, and the Montana venture is apparently
finished. Anyway the conclusion is up to you. If it helps, I tend
to go with either or both, depending on the rest of the soil mix.
Perlite is good for a heavier clay soil and vermiculite for a sandier
one that needs more water retention. Finally, if you're working
with either one a lot, wear a mask to avoid breathing in the dust.

Otherwise it's easy enough to stand upwind and avoid inhaling it by the cloud-load.

If you do make your own mix, keep a record of what you used in what proportions. If it's a winner you'll probably want to repeat it. Continually tweaking the recipe to come up with the perfect blend is part of the container farming fun.

Pots a plenty

You can use anything for a container as long as it holds the growing medium, accepts and drains water and gives the plant space to grow. You are not required to buy expensive pots from the pot section of the garden center, although they may look nicer than plastic pickle buckets. On the other hand, plastic pickle buckets can be visually interesting too, depending on the kind of look you're after. If it doesn't have them already, drill drainage holes into the sides of whatever container you use about half an inch up from the bottom. Only the very diligent grower should attempt keeping a pot properly irrigated without drainage holes — although it can be done if you carefully add just the right amount at the right times to avoid the extremes of flooding and drought.

Message in a bottle

Or you could use a design from Shouichi Taniguchi of the Midori-Ryu Seikatsu environmental group in Ichinomiya, Japan. At the global conference on biodiversity in Nagoya in 2010, Taniguchi's group taught visitors how to make vegetable bottles, which are simple enough to create on the go and use a resource so plentiful — plastic pop bottles — that the world will never run out of potential containers.

Taniguchi cuts the narrow tops off the bottles and puts an absorbing layer of peat moss on the bottom (you could substitute coir, or if you don't have it try going with just gravel or pebbles). He threads a strip of non-woven fabric such as a dish cloth or

みどりりゅう
緑流生活
A Midori style is good living
for people and the planet.

Vegetable Bottle
ベジボトル

The Vegetable is grow
with the PET bottle.

Japanese paper
or
Nonwoven fabric

Pipe
The excess fluid evaporates
with this pipe, and air is sent.

The root rot doesn't do.

Bog moss

Another nifty idea from Japan.

absorbent paper through a straw and places it into the bottle so the fabric sticks out of both sides, one end into the bottom of the bottle and the other end out the top of the straw into the air. Then he adds compost with organic fertilizer and plants a vegetable seed on top. And that's it. With no drainage holes, the vegetable bottle can go anywhere indoors, and even be moved around to sunny spots during the day without worry about oozing out a muddy mess. The straw and fabric wick away excess moisture so you won't drown your plant with too much water. They also bring oxygen down to the root area, which helps the plant grow. Taniguchi has found the vegetable bottles to be a hit, especially with kids because they can create their own mini-farm in less than an hour and take home a handful of healthy-food-to-be.

SOME THINGS TO CONSIDER BEFORE BUYING CONTAINERS

- Do you have to buy or can you recycle?
- Bigger is better to hold moisture and give roots room to grow.
- "Self-watering" types can reduce watering chores.
- Proper drainage is necessary to avoid waterlogging.
- Rolling containers may allow multi-functions in a small space.

Or perhaps you don't even need a pot-like container. A bag of soil is still soil. Simply slit the top open and plant away.

Size matters in container choices because the more growing medium you can offer the less meticulous you'll need to be in keeping it properly irrigated (smaller amounts of soil dry sooner, especially on windy days). The root systems of plants have also evolved to grow to a certain size, which you can restrict but only to a degree. A fairly sizeable vegetable plant like squash or eggplant can be grown in a five-gallon container. In a one-gallon container you could probably get away with two or maybe three carrots. Greens such as lettuce, spinach and salad blends can be grown in surprisingly small containers or even shallow trays, especially if you pick when young to use as cut-and-come-again crops.

Virtually anything you can grow in the ground you can grow in a pot, if you remember to think like a plant and provide the essentials.

Potted herbs

The Mediterranean types do well in containers since they tend to thrive in hot and dry conditions. Choices include basil, marjoram, summer and winter savory, thyme and oregano and more. Small pots are fine if they have a width and depth of at least 4–5 inches (10–12 centimeters), although larger pots will permit plants to grow larger if you're hoping to grow a lot to dry for use throughout the year.

Shrubbier herbs such as bay, juniper, lavender, lemon verbena, sage and tarragon do well in pots at least 9 inches (23 centimeters) in diameter and depth.

Potentially taller herbs such as anise hyssop, fennel and sweet cicely work in pots that are 18 inches (45 centimeters) in diameter and depth, but may need staking to stay upright.

Chives, lemon balm, mints and parsley do fine in pots, and will be healthiest if you provide them with a rich, well-draining medium you remember to keep well-watered.

Shallow containers including seed trays can be sown with caraway, dill, coriander and many other types of herbs to be cut in the seedling stage.

Potted vegetables

Practically any vegetable you like can be grown in a container. Members of the *Solanaceae* family such as eggplant, tomatoes and peppers might even prefer the added heat a sun-absorbing container can provide. People have grown beans, cabbage, kale and garlic in pots. Salad greens are easy to grow in all kinds of containers of all kinds of sizes, as are spinach and watercress. Strawberries in a terracotta pot with multiple layered openings make a classic food garden container.

Potted fruit

Fruit trees in containers can provide a striking visual boost to any balcony farm. Again the Mediterranean types are often hardy enough to stand the abuse they may be subjected to in a limited growing space. Try olives, figs, medlars, mulberry, grapes and citruses such as orange, lemon and lime. Of course you'll need

COMMON CONTAINER PLANT PROBLEMS

- Tall spindly plants: insufficient sun or nitrogen.
- Yellow from bottom, poor color: excessive water, low fertility.
- Plants wilt even with water: poor drainage and aeration.
- Marginal burning or firing of leaves: salt buildup in need of flush with water.
- Stunted or sickly plant: low temperature, low phosphates.
- Holes in leaves: insects.
- Leaves with spots, dead areas, powdery or rusty areas: diseases.

to consider winter wherever you live, either providing protection on the balcony with a cover and/or heating elements such as old style, big-bulb Christmas lights or by overwintering in a protected space such as a garage or even a living room. Hardy fruits that can usually stay outside (and may need the chilling hours to bear fruit the next summer) include apple, pear, cherry, currant, peach, blueberry and nectarine. Also consider less common choices such as persimmon, pawpaw and loquat.

Potted flowers

Grow edible flowers for pleasing views you can also eat. Varieties to try include chrysanthemums, daylilies, borage, fuchsias, nasturtiums, pansies, pelargoniums (geraniums), marigolds, violets and roses. The petals can be added to pancakes and waffles, soups and salads, ice cubes, jellies, cakes and teas.

Just watch me

Because your balcony farm is so close, you will be diligent in your daily inspections to remove pests such as aphids before they can establish a beachhead and start claiming leaf territory for their side. On your daily rounds you can also remove weeds, trim dead leaves and flowers, train vines and give your plants a gentle shake as you talk to them. Even if you don't believe in the positive results of human-plant conversations, you mechanistic cad, that gentle shake is said to help strengthen the stems much the way winds would do in a natural setting.

Bag one

MSGs (multistory gardens) are an ambitious name for the cereal sacks used in refugee camps in Africa by people with no land, tools, supplies or much of anything else, although they do have a dire need for nutritious food (anemia levels for women and children at two camps in Kenya were found to be above 70 percent). Reports in the RUAF's *Urban Agriculture Magazine* about MSGs introduced by the World Food Programme and the United Nations High Commission of Refugees find the sacks work not only to grow needed food but also to provide employment and a sense of empowerment—two more things also lacking among refugees.

Materials: one empty 50-kg cereal bag and several empty tin cans.

Method: Drill drainage holes in the sides and bottoms of the cans, leaving the bottom of one can intact. Fill the cans with stones and stack on top of each other in the middle of the standing bag, starting with the one with the solid bottom. Fill the space around the cans inside the bag with a blend of compost and organic fertilizer. Plant the top of the bag with vegetable seeds. When the plants emerge, thin by transplanting some into slots you cut into

Walk This Way

Examples & Inspiration

The Klondike gold rush drew tens of thousands of would-be miners, very few of whom, it turned out, ever struck it rich. The ones who did make out like bandits were the outfitters and equipment suppliers. There might be something in that lesson for urban agriculture, which now has its own store in Washington, D.C., called Urban Sustainable. Manager and cofounder Matt Doherty says the store sells hydroponic systems, organic seeds, nutrients, home composting systems and more. "There is such a disconnection right now regarding our food supply," he notes, adding the new store is looking into holding workshops on home farming and creating a healthier local food system.

— urbansustainable.org —

the sides of the bag. Or grow taller plants (tomato, eggplant) on top and leafy greens in the layered slots. Irrigate by pouring about five liters of water into the top can (refugees often use graywater left over from washing).

Aquaponics

The idea behind aquaponics can be alluring to anyone who likes systems, cycles, fresh vegetables and fish together in a gurgling display of nature and technology that may also be strikingly beautiful.

Aquaponics combines fish cultivation in water (aquaculture) with soil-less plant growing (hydroponics). Think of hooking your fish tank up to a pump that circulates the water to a pot holding edible plants. The fish poo fertilizes the plants and the plants filter the fish water, so everyone wins. Well, everyone who isn't a fish or the plant, as they get eaten — but the system is set up to keep them healthy to the point where they become big and delicious.

That's the ideal, in a small and simple operation anyone with a little experience in aquarium keeping could set up at home. It may not be all that easy to reach at the higher production scale, for

---

SIX REASONS TO TRY AN AQUAPONICS SYSTEM

1. Harvest organic vegetables year-round.

2. Raise fresh, toxin-free fish that won't diminish the ocean's supply.

3. Systems can be anywhere — in a basement, on a driveway, on land unsuitable for growing.

4. The environmental impact is low—no waste water dumped into local waterways.

5. You can practice resource conservation (using one-sixth the water of conventional agriculture).

6. Enjoy the educational appeal of an ecosystem in action.

first-timers. I'm speaking here not from personal experience but observing others who have tried. It seems to be not uncommon for newcomers to kill their young fish. Not that they're irresponsible people. They meticulously test the water to determine the pH, ammonia and nitrite levels and so on, but it is a tiny ecosystem they're creating, for plants and creatures that evolution did not create to find themselves together in a tub in a Boise garage, where even a little change in the chemical balance can have big consequences. It's also worth noting that the setbacks are usually seen as just that, setbacks, not deterrents that should stop anyone from trying again until they get it right.

If you're going to get into aquaculture you should probably be prepared to tinker and troubleshoot and repair. "You get really good at fixing pumps," explained the guy who helps keep the Growing Power organization's aquaculture operation going in

Jody Peters' list of materials for a small aquaponics operation:
- 10-gallon aquarium
- grow bed (plastic storage container approx. 20" × 12" × 4–6" deep)
- pump (40–60 gph capacity)
- hose (make sure it fits your pump)
- hose clamps (to fit pump, stainless steel)
- T-fitting (same diameter as hose)
- growing medium (hydroton, gravel, perlite)
- air pump/stone

Tools:
- drill
- ⅜" bit for drainage holes
- 1⁄16" to 3⁄32" bit for growing bed, tubing holes
- ½"–1" bit for hose/tubing entry
- flathead screwdriver

Approximate cost: $120

Milwaukee. Setbacks didn't stop him either: the Growing Power greenhouses were crammed with fish tanks and crops.

Why go to all the trouble of tending a finicky crop like fish? Because they're an excellent protein source that can be raised anywhere, they taste great, and they sell for good money. Tilapia, a favorite fish of aquaculturists because they eat everything, grow fast and are not finicky about water quality, cost Growing Power eight cents a fry, but sell at their market for six dollars a fish. With a 500-gallon tank (picture something big enough to hold you and a dozen of your supermodel friends) the thumbnail rule of one gallon per fish suggests you could raise 500 tilapia.

Not to mention all the fresh tasty greens on top. Watercress, which is fantastic raw or steamed or stir-fried, is an excellent choice, but people also go with lettuce, various Asian greens that end with "choy" or whatever they really like.

School of fish

I went to see an aquaponics operation at Vancouver's Windemere High School that wasn't growing a lot, unless you count the minds of our brightest kids as something worth cultivating. In a greenhouse in the middle of the campus courtyard which they had turned into an organic farm, the highschoolers had built an aquaponics system with an impressively fangled pump and recovery system that seemed to rely on gravity and duct tape, yet actually worked. The vegetable section had a healthy tomato and a few edible greens, but their fish of choice was…goldfish. Not much there in the way of meals, but they were using the little pets as a test case while exploring the possibility of raising koi, a potentially valuable item that could be sold for more than tilapia or catfish or perch.

Jody Peters from the Backyard Bounty Collective in Vancouver offers workshops that include a supplies list for a small balcony-sized system that can help newcomers determine if aquaculture is in their blood.

The design below is from Growing Power in Milwaukee, which is big on aquaculture. They grow fish to sell and to show aspiring farmers how they can too. The system would be too heavy for a typical balcony, but is included to give builders ideas on how the setup works: once you have the basic idea, the sizing can be changed to accommodate your space and interests, not to mention your ability to keep all the living parts living.

Finally, you don't have to build a system from scratch to be a fish and veggie aquaponics farmer. There are companies that will sell you the entire operation outright. The Nelson and Pade aquaponics supplies firm out of Wisconsin has systems in sizes from demonstration to what-are-we-going-to-do-with-a-ton-of-fish-and-lettuce? Its Home Garden model is made up of four 50-gallon tanks and a 4' × 6' raft tank for the plants. You would need about 12' × 24' of room for the equipment and walking-around space. It costs $5,795, with an extra $500 or so if you want lighting. They also offer a comprehensive website with helpful information on all things aquaponics (aquaponics.com). Another site with a raft of information for newcomers is Backyard Aquaponics: (backyard aquaponics.com).

TAKE HOME MESSAGE

The seed knows what to do.

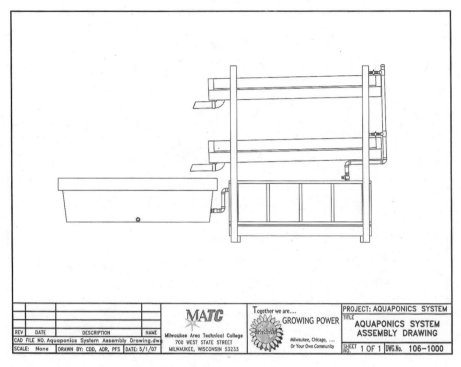

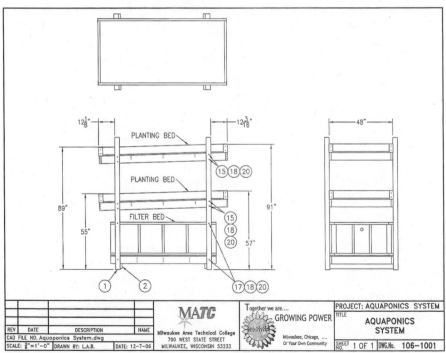

Aquaponics system design courtesy of the Growing Power organization.

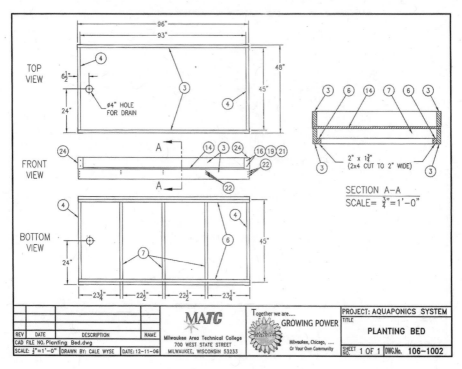

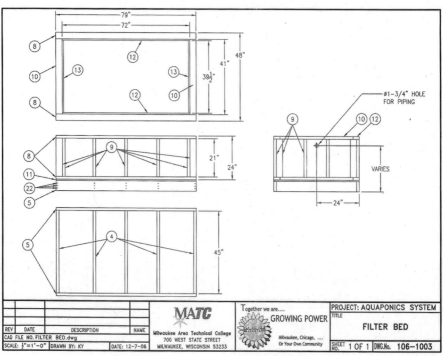

Item #	Quantity	Description	Material	Sub-Assembly
1	4	4" x 4" x 8'	Lumber	Aquaponics System Main Assembly
2	2	2" x 4" x 55"	Lumber	Aquaponics System Main Assembly
3	8	2" x 6" x 8'	Lumber	Planting Bed
4	13	2" x 6" x 45"	Lumber	Planting Bed and Filter Bed
5	2	2" x 6" x 79"	Lumber	Filter Bed
6	4	2" x 1-1/2" x 93"	Lumber	Planting Bed
7	6	2" x 4" x 45"	Lumber	Planting Bed
8	4	2" x 4" x 79"	Lumber	Filter Bed
9	22	2" x 4" x 21"	Lumber	Filter Bed
10	4	2" x 4" x 41"	Lumber	Filter Bed
11	1	48" x 79" x 3/4" Plywood	Plywood	Filter Bed
12	2	24" x 72" x 3/4" Plywood	Plywood	Filter Bed
13	2	24" x 39-1/2" Plywood	Plywood	Filter Bed
14	2	4' x 8' x 3/4" Plywood	Plywood	Planting Bed
15	16	1/2" x 6" Long, Carriage Bolt	Steel	Aquaponics System Main Assembly
16	40	5/16" x 2" Long, Carriage Bolt	Steel	All
17	8	1/2" x 9" long, Carriage Bolt	Steel	Aquaponics System Main Assembly
18	48	1/2" Flat Washer	Steel	All
19	16	5/16" Flat Washer	Steel	All
20	48	1/2" Hex Nut	Steel	All
21	16	5/16" Hex Nut	Steel	All
22	214	3" Deck Screws	Steel	All
23	144	1-1/2" Deck Screws, used for attaching plywood to frame	Steel	All
24	8	3" x 3" x 3/16" - 6" Long, Corner	Angle Iron	Planting Bed
		EPDM, 45 mils thick, Liner for planting beds and filter beds, available from Nursery, Pet Shop, Building Supply, and Pond Supply stores.	EPDM	Planting Bed and Filter Bed
		Caulk for planting beds drain	100% Silicone	Planting Bed

CHAPTER 3

EDIBLE ESTATES
ADDING FOOD TO HOME GARDEN DESIGN

For those who want a taste of urban agriculture, to see if they like it before they buy the whole farm idea, the best place to begin may be with a portion of the backyard.

You can grow a surprising amount and variety of crops and still keep the features of a typical yard, say because you like the look and function of your lawn and patio and lunar-landing-module-sized barbecue. In the next chapter we'll look deeper into why you may want to sod off altogether when it comes to grass. For this chapter, let's just say you can have your features, even the lawn darts, and eat your homegrown food too.

Fair warning: this may be the beginning of your descent into a serious farm fixation. That small patch of sugar snap peas may look nice, and just wait until you taste their burst of vivacity straight off the vine, but consider it a drug. If you open this door, you should walk through knowing you may be tempted to grow more, and this feeling may gnaw at you until you take up the entire backyard, and then the front, and then go looking for even more land to plow. Don't say you haven't been warned.

Beauty and the bean

A key message of this chapter: food as it is grown is not ugly. Farmers and other plant people know this already. The push of new seedlings up through the surface of the earth, the height and breadth of the intricate green designs of growing plants seeking light, flowers offering undetected aromas and stunning visuals to entice winged pollinators, the color and swell of fruit as it matures, even the final stages of seed production and plant decay — all have their own inherent beauty that can draw the eye and stir the soul. So let us briefly pause to reflect sadly on the city people who can see none of this. And then get to work creating pockets of edible beauty.

Expect these food patches to become more common as urban agriculture grows more popular, by choice or need. We can help the transition by growing food that is visible, accessible, interesting and beautiful. So don't think you must hide your vegetables behind the dahlias and roses. Give your food and food-growing expertise the prominence they deserve, starting with a prime portion of your backyard.

Edible landscaping

Potager is a French word for kitchen gardens, derived from their original role: providing pot herbs for soup or "potage." Some of the more famous examples lean toward the prim and proper, bringing a refined sense of style to plants some might otherwise consider coarse or frumpy.

You'll need to buy that European castle you've been considering before trying to match the extravaganza of the Château de Villandry in the Loire Valley, France, but until then you can borrow ideas from how elegantly it blends vegetables into a garden design (chateauvillandry.fr/). Originally created by medieval monks, the site now includes a Music Garden and a Love Garden, nothing wrong with either of those, but the most prominent space is still devoted to a hectare (2.5 acres) of food planted in geometrically arrayed squares of contrasting colors. In a positive move, the garden is gradually being returned to organic growing methods, something the ancient monks would recognize.

Château de Villandry was also said to provide inspiration for the late Rosemary Verey's smaller *potager* at Barnsley House. Verey became a noted gardening expert in part by designing her own property in Gloucestershire which is still visited by aficionados today. The entire site takes up 4.5 acres. The *potager* portion is not much bigger than a tennis court, but is much admired and copied for its displays blending, for instance, the colors of edible and ornamental cabbages.

These examples are mentioned not because I think you should try to mimic them (*ornamental* cabbage?), but to help some get over the mindset of vegetables as ugly. This includes city officials stuck in the previous century's paradigm of just what a city can and should be. It requires a measure of independent thinking for preferences to shift from brush-cut lawns to living ecosystems demonstrating the nature we co-create, so it may come as no surprise that civic bureaucrats will be among the last to get it.

Site lines

Give your vegetables the sunniest spot. Shade should be reserved for plants that like it, and for rain barrels, compost bins, tool sheds and the like.

SEVEN REASONS TO GROW VEGETABLES IN A BACKYARD PLOT

1. Discover food as more than a consumer product.
2. Get dinner ideas by looking out the window.
3. Nearby crops are easy to water and watch for pests.
4. Food plants enhance a backyard garden design.
5. Show friends and neighbors how to eat a landscape.
6. Pick vegetables and herbs for the barbecue just steps away.
7. A productive patch can increase your property value.

The closer you place your food area to general backyard traffic, the more likely you'll be to tend it. All the better if it can be clearly seen from the kitchen window. Grow your vegetables in a sunny, convenient and attractive place and you might be able to avoid the curiosity I see every year, in which people toil for hours over their crops in spring and summer only to let the produce ripen and rot due to neglect in fall. I'm not sure of the psychology behind this odd phenomenon, but I've done it myself. It could be due to different energies in different seasons that sometimes just don't match up. I don't know, but it makes me think we should be more in tune with the entire cycle of growing food rather than seeing it as something we can just plant and then ignore.

Start small

Beginners are often enthused, which is understandable, and certainly not to be discouraged: Shunryu Suzuki wrote an entire book about the value of keeping a fresh outlook because, "In the beginner's mind there are many possibilities, in the expert's mind

Compare the size of the lettuce plants inside and outside the cold frame.

there are few." But it can be counterproductive to take on more than you can handle for the first season. Growing food is work. Look at farmers: they're not lazy people. When you grow food, you have to keep up all the time. Your plants, and the weeds and pests, don't take breaks. So rather than risk burnout from taking too big a bite to start, consider building up your farm in manageable stages.

Growing is seasonal but you can also view it strategically as a lifelong pursuit, and pace yourself accordingly. I often tell people who attend one of our grafting workshops, in which they fuse a heritage apple variety onto a dwarf rootstock, that patience is a virtue. Still they ask, "When will I get apples?" I explain that their energy, and the tree's, should be focused not on an early harvest but on developing a solid branch structure that will provide abundant fruit for many years to come. They nod, weakly, until I add, "You'll start getting a few apples in a couple of years," and then they're happy. It may be the same with your backyard venture: even a small patch will provide you with food this growing season, while serving as a base for greater things to come.

Build it and they will grow.

A single 4' × 8' vegetable bed will be enough to engage, develop a grasp of basic growing techniques and produce food that will make you proud. That's a reasonable size even the over-busy should be able to maintain, but if you know you're the stick-to-it type, and you're committed to growing good food in a better world, go ahead and make your plot bigger. You can always get friends or the food bank to help you eat the excess harvest.

Raise your game

Building a raised bed for your food crops takes a little money and time, but can be worth it, especially for a limited space like a backyard.

As (one-day) agriculture expert Stephen Colbert explained in a speech before a US Congressional committee in support of the United Farm Workers Union: "Please don't make me do this again. It is really, really hard. For one thing, picking beans you have to spend all day bending over. It turns out—and I did not know this—most soil is at ground level. If we can put a man on the Moon why can't we make the earth waist high?"

Choose wood that will last. Cedar and redwood cost more than spruce, pine or fir, but you'll save money over the long run on replacement costs. Long after your pine box would have rotted away, a frame built from cedar, which contains its own natural fungicide, will still be standing. The cheapest alternative is the one you do not want. Pressure-treated wood is not recommended where food will be grown. The chemicals used to preserve the wood will leach into the soil, and perhaps get taken up by your plants and then by you when you eat them. Some people, like the sales guy at the hardware store, may insist it's no longer a problem because the old method of treating wood that used CCA (chromated copper arsenate) which was banned by the US Environmental Protection Agency has been replaced with ACQ (alkaline copper quat) and CA-B (copper azole). But the jury is still out on how safe these alternatives really are. Copper, which is included to repel insects, is a heavy metal that can reach toxic levels in the soil. They may not get that high from a planter box, but why take the chance when there are natural alternatives?

Or even unnatural alternatives. Recycled plastic lumber is an option that sounds kitschy, costs twice as much as cedar and leaves curls of plastic when you cut it. But hang on, there's a good side. The plastic turns out to be harder than you might expect, looking as if it might indeed last twice as long as cedar, as the manufacturer claims. It also takes an environmental negative, plastic waste, and turns it into a positive. The black version I used for a community garden project was reclaimed from printer toner cartridges that would otherwise have been trucked to the landfill. And two years later it still looks good. With a little mud and scuffing, no one will even notice your plastic isn't wood unless they try to carve their initials into it.

Simple box

A planter box can be simple or fancy. Designs for boxes of all stripes and sizes can be found for free on the internet. Or make up your own—you're really just putting up walls to hold in soil,

EIGHT ADVANTAGES TO RAISED VEGETABLE BEDS

1. Warmer soil lengthens the growing season.
2. Confined areas are easier to keep weed-free.
3. You can grow above poor or toxic soil.
4. Get precise control over soil ingredients.
5. You will never need to walk on, and thus compact, the soil.
6. Excellent drainage.
7. Less bending.
8. Raised beds look good.

so the options are open. Nail four pieces of wood together into a rectangle and you have a planter box. Stack rectangles of the same dimensions on top to extend the height of your box. If you do go with this bare-bones style, it's worth adding reinforcements at the corners and the middles of sides longer than six feet to prevent the walls from separating or bending over time. Screw or nail the sides to vertical pieces of two-by-four or four-by-four in each corner and the center of long pieces.

Or you can go with fancier designs, using tongue-and-groove joinery at the corners and beveled paneling for the walls and whatever else strikes your woodworking fancy.

On any kind of planting box if you screw galvanized plumber's metal stripping to the sides it will hold a half-inch PVC pipe you can bend in an arc to the other side, then cover with removable plastic sheeting to form a mini-greenhouse.

The Woodworkers Institute, a website created by a British woodworkers' publishing company, offers plans for a surprisingly attractive planter made with used pallets. It looks better than it sounds, and only costs about £5 worth of materials, but does require a certain level of skill and interest in carpentry — the design calls for tenon and mortise fittings. If those words mean nothing to you, stick with something simpler (woodworkersinstitute.com /page.asp?p=884).

Uber-box

When you build a raised bed you don't have to limit yourself to just the raised bed. Add a 10-inch plank around the perimeter on top for bench seating. Or attach a bench that lifts up to reveal a small toolbox for a hose and a few trowels. Or add a trellis to the back that can support climbing vegetables like peas or beans. Or add four-by-four posts to serve as the supports for an arbor of grape or kiwi vines. Or combine all of the above. This simple design made with free 3D software available on the internet adds

A raised bed can include a lock box and a bench and a trellis and an arbor.

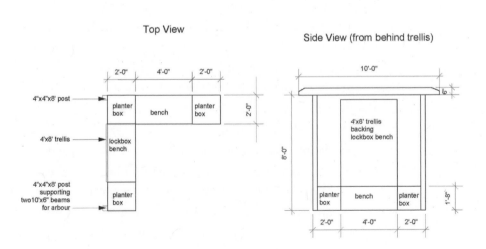

Planter box + bench+ lockbox + trellis + arbor

two seating benches (one of which holds a storage box for tools), three planter boxes, a trellis and an arbor.

The big organic

Once you've located your planting space, in the ground or a raised bed, you're ready to prepare the soil. Organically, of course, right? If so, let's agree on just what that means.

You have probably seen it described in markets as "certified organic." Standards are of course a good thing, otherwise "organic" might be like "sustainable," an easy word for even the most heinous politician or developer to use in justifying some plunder. But organic certification typically involves a three-year process and inspections and fees and more paperwork than some farmers care to fill out, so there are commercial growers who just don't bother, even though they use natural fertilizers and don't spray poisons.

I could come up with statistics on pesticides to make the organic or no-spray approach seem not only desirable but the only logical choice for the environment. Such as: the US Department of Agriculture found the residues of pesticides in seven out of ten fruits and vegetables tested. The most dosed contained a toxic cocktail of thirteen different kinds of pesticides. I mention this not to scare you into washing your produce a little more vigorously: these tests were conducted on fruit and vegetables as they are commonly eaten, which means the bananas were checked after being peeled and broccoli after being washed.

So, yes, organic is good, and the right choice if you have one, even though the organic brand may have lost a little of its luster recently with mega-farms and big corporations getting into the game. For consumers, the decision typically comes down to availability and affordability and quality. Most people I know shop on both sides of the fence, although less on the costlier organic side. But when it comes to growing, we're all organic. And that's what I recommend to anyone beginning to grow their own food.

Lively up yourself

For newcomers, I offer this simple definition of organic farming: growing without synthetic fertilizers or pesticides. I explain why we don't want to use artificial products in our living soil, adding something about their war origins with the surplus of ammonia from bombs, and poisons from chemical weapons, which marketers somehow convinced suburbanites to pour on their lawns.

But I don't dwell on the things that being organic means you *don't* do. Instead I tell them about the things you *do* do. Beginning with the fact that it isn't newfangled or trendy but rather the way people have been growing food for ten thousand years. It's only in the last century that the really newfangled and strange idea of adding chemical synthetics to the soil appeared.

I think of organic on a personal level as being less about certification and more of a philosophy or an ethic. Not quite rigid, not exactly a solid line between good and bad, but rather a positive. It stems from being alive. We choose things that support life. Organic means working with the natural ecosystems of your site. It aims to achieve a harmony with nature, balancing inputs and outputs, recognizing the important cycles of nutrients, treating plants as part of a flow rather than a linear product to be zapped and dosed and collected at the end.

An organic approach to soil means recognizing that it is alive. Organic farming is a long-term venture, where soil is not simply a base in which to hold things but an ecological site itself, connected to all things around it. Organic methods, based on being alive, require an understanding of the supporting interconnections. Coincidentally, this is precisely the thing on which urban agriculture of the future will be based: healthy networks.

Old school organics

Harold Steves learned how to grow on his family farm in Richmond, across the Fraser River from Vancouver, and in studying agricultural sciences at the University of British Columbia. Steves has gone on to become a hero to many in the province for his steadfast career in farming and in politics supporting farmers. He was key to the creation of BC's Agricultural Land Reserve (ALR), one of the most progressive farmland protection policies in North America. Steves says his family farm, started by his pioneering great-grandfather in 1877, has long been organic by default.

"Everyone comes to me and says, 'Wow, we just learned about organic agriculture. How come you're doing it?' I would say because I never learned how *not* to do it. We always rotated our crops and that took care of things."

But didn't he learn modern farming practices at UBC?

"Oh, absolutely. But you get different mentors. My father as a mentor never used chemicals. When I went to UBC it was the height of what they called the Green Revolution. I took a course on the use of herbicides and pesticides. They didn't even have a textbook on it at that time. All the information was put out by Canadian Industries, Ltd. from Trail, that took all the oil and coal to manufacture all these chemicals. But in my graduating year I was a teaching assistant to a Dr. Mackenzie whom everyone ridiculed. Dr. Mackenzie was from the old school. He rejected all this stuff. He was the last professor for twenty or thirty years to teach organic agriculture there. I was his teaching assistant and all I was doing assisting him was what we were doing on the farm. Here I was in this course assisting him and teaching organic agriculture while I had to pass the other course in weed control pesticides. I remember once being told by one of the professors, maybe it was weed control, the reason many of the farms had not survived into the '50s and '60s was that they had not embraced pesticides. Well, those farms that embraced pesticides and herbicides are all gone but we're still here."

Steves' effort to bring the ALR to the province in the 1970s stopped the movement toward huge farms that swept the rest of the continent because it was no longer profitable to buy farmland to build factory farms. One result that is seldom recognized is healthier food for the province's consumers.

"BC farmers, even the ones that used herbicides and pesticides, because they were small farms and they rotated their crops, never became factory farms and therefore never depleted their soil. So if you buy food from any farmer in BC you're getting soil that's much more nutritious than anything that could be imported from these factory farms, because the farmers have always rotated their crops. They might use chemicals, they might use Roundup and things like that, but on a much more limited scale compared to the factory farms in the United States and Mexico and other parts of the world. So locally grown food from any farm in British Columbia will be more nutritious than imported food. It's as simple as that."

Steves finds the message he was trying to get across to young farm students five decades ago hasn't changed all that much.

"Now, why organic? Well, basically organic, you avoid even the trace chemicals from the fertilizers and sprays and hormones. On organic farms the only way you can grow food is to use manures and compost and to rotate your crops. And that takes me back to where I started. That's what we're teaching now at the urban Farm School [an urban agricultural program the city of Richmond supports by offering incubator farmland for several years to graduates]. We're looking at reeducating a new generation of young

FIVE REASONS TO GROW ORGANIC FOOD

1. It tastes better.
2. It's better for you.
3. A dollar's worth of seeds can produce hundreds of dollar's worth of food.
4. You'll work, sweat, ache… and feel alive.
5. You can claim your rightful place as an ally of the Earth.

farmers that will be able to replenish the land to produce more wholesome food and get higher production than you can from chemical crops. That's another thing people don't understand. The reason the industrial farm is successful is that they've been able to have vast acreages and produce huge crops at large profit. But you can produce much more nutrition per acre with organic farming than with factory farming."

Soil 101

The secret to growing healthy food lies at your feet, in healthy soil. Good farmers know they're really growing the soil that grows the plants.

Note I use the term "soil" rather than "dirt." Soil is the source of all life, and a wondrous and fascinating thing. Dirt is something annoying that won't come out in the wash. I have been sure never to confuse the two since the day one of my landscape architecture professors, grilling me on a design that was half-baked at best, wearily asked what material I had proposed for a pathway running through the site. I looked at the unlabeled space, drew a blank, then replied, "Dirt?" The wince he shot back at hearing the word was enough to convince me to never take soil for granted again.

What is soil? Pick up a handful. Don't be afraid. It won't hurt you, it washes out later (or sooner, if you remembered to put lotion on your hands before heading out to work the crops), and you'll know you're on your way to becoming a bona fide farmer when you share their love of touching, hefting, sifting and smelling soil.

Rock on

Typically about half of what you're holding will be rock. These minerals are a combination of clay, silt and sand, with more of one or another giving the soil its most recognizable characteristics in color and water-holding capacity. A heavy clay soil holds together if you squeeze a wet handful in your fist. A light sandy soil crumbles under the same test, while a silty soil is somewhere in between. One quarter of your handful of soil will be air pockets and another quarter will be water. The remainder, just 2 to 5 percent of the total, consists of organic matter, all the living and decaying things that mean your soil is alive. If 5 percent doesn't sound like much, consider that your single handful of soil contains more living organisms than there are people on Earth.

This is where plants derive their essential nutrients. The main ones, which you see listed on fertilizer bags, are nitrogen, phosphorus and potassium, also known as N-P-K. There are also many micronutrients, tiny in comparison but necessary because their absence can screw up the growing process. Plants are what they absorb, including these micronutrients, just as we are we eat.

Something's rotten

Of course you have a compost bin in your yard in which you recycle all your uncooked food scraps along with grass clippings and garden waste, right? If not, you should know home compost is the most Earth-conscious way to get healthy soil-amending materials without involving the transportation system or money. Every bucket of waste you compost is one less bucket that must be hauled to the dump, saving everyone money and the atmosphere from more greenhouse gas emissions. If you don't already compost, it's easy to get started.

Keep a covered bucket under your kitchen sink to collect vegetable and fruit peels, coffee grounds and tea leaves, eggshells and any other uncooked food scraps you produce (but no meat or fish that might entice critters). A plastic ice-cream bucket will work, although a metal pail with a lid is less likely to absorb smells and easier to clean. Every few days, or sooner if your bucket fills up, dump it into your compost bin or pile.

Your compost should be a mix of materials, nitrogen and carbon, to keep the process going. This doesn't mean you need a science degree to make it work. Just try to add roughly equal amounts of the two, which can be thought of in terms of nitrogen-green-wet and carbon-brown-dry. (The proportion of carbon to nitrogen can actually be much higher, but it's probably easier to remember to go with roughly equal amounts.) So when you add a bucket of nitrogen-green-wet in the form of kitchen scraps, add a few handfuls of carbon-brown-dry in the form of fallen leaves or dried lawn clippings or shredded paper, covering the wet gunky stuff to deter flies. Turning your pile regularly will introduce oxygen, which is important to keep the process going. If it smells bad, it means it's gone anaerobic, or oxygen-less, so turn it to get it back on track. Finished compost is dark, crumbly and smells like the good sweet earth itself.

People who compost are often aghast at anyone who doesn't, but it's a bigger issue than a few recalcitrant neighbors. We're generally behind in North America, especially in how we handle waste at the neighborhood level. In Lahore, Pakistan, 40 percent of the city's waste is collected by farmers for animal feed and as a soil amendment. Mexico City uses over half its sewage to fertilize alfalfa fields, with the crop then sold in shops to backyard livestock producers who, in turn, sell the manure to urban growers of vegetables and flowers.

Keep the grass off

To convert a large section of lawn from primped-up grass to productive vegetable growing space, you may want to rent a sod cutter at your local tool rental place. It will do a clean job of stripping the layer of grass off at the root, leaving the bare soil behind. But you can tackle a smaller space with a spade and some grunt work. Cut into and lift the grass a piece at a time, shaking off the clinging soil before you toss the scalp into the compost.

Or easier still, you can avoid digging into the grass entirely by using the sheet mulch method. Also known as lasagna gardening, it's one way to practise no-till growing.

Five steps to sheet mulching

1. Mow the grassy area to be converted as low as possible.
2. If it doesn't drain well, poke a spading fork under the grass into the soil to open up passages.
3. Dig out any weeds such as morning glory that could survive the imminent cover-up process.
4. Cover the area with overlapping pieces of cardboard or six to eight layers of newspaper, then wet thoroughly.
5. Cover the cardboard with alternating layers of nitrogen and carbon. For example, an inch or two of manure, topped by dried leaves, topped by kitchen scraps, topped by straw, and so on until you reach your desired height. Higher is better, and three feet would be good-sized pile to start (it will shrink), but you can go with something smaller as well. You can also add to the pile as it breaks down, remembering to top it each time with a dry carbon layer to discourage flies from feeding and laying eggs. You can also cover the pile with black plastic, which will help warm the contents and encourage decomposition, but straw or burlap sacks may look nicer.

In about six months, depending on the weather and what you've added, the materials should have broken down well enough to no longer be recognizable, which means you can plant in it.

Or, if you want to grow sooner than that, like this weekend, add about six inches of soil on top of the cardboard/newspapers and plant right away. The layers of paper and grass beneath will eventually break down.

Plant the menu

What food crops to grow is one of the delightful puzzles you will enjoy solving every year. You can start by rephrasing the question. What food do you love to eat? Pick some of your favorite fresh produce and see if local garden stores sell the seeds—a good clue to whether it will grow in your area. Nearby gardeners or garden store staff will also tell you if your climate zone is amenable, although, with the way the world is going, someone is going to clean up capturing the homegrown pineapple market in New York.

Easy crops to think of first for a good chance at a successful harvest include beans, beets, garlic, lettuce, radish, spinach and squash. I list those names knowing that "easy" is relative depending on the year, the region and the individual site. I grew tons of beets in one Vancouver lot, but got skunked with the same seed in another a year later. Ditto for the spinach, only in reverse. So don't be discouraged if you don't get a bumper crop on your first try. Any professional farmer can tell you sad tales of wipeouts in bad years.

Mushroom among us

If keep-it-simple struck you as sound advice in sizing your vegetable patch, you may be intrigued by the lure of mushrooms. They are a fine example of a crop that wants little more than a leg up to do all the work for you. They don't even ask for a sunny spot; because they're fungi, lacking the chlorophyll of green plants, they rely for food on other plant material, such as logs, tree stumps, bark mulch or soil. If you have a backyard big enough to include a woody area, you may already have a mushroom farm in the making.

You still have to get the spawn, which may require some searching to find a local mushroom grower who also sells start-up materials. You also need to provide the proper host for the type of mushroom you're after. Oyster mushrooms are popular with beginners because they'll grow on a variety of surfaces. Shiitake (pronounced SHE-tah-kay) are another favorite among fungi fans.

If you're growing these delectables for your own table, you can inoculate your outdoor mini-farm and pretty much ignore it until the fruiting bodies are ready to be picked. If you're growing for

The Strathcona Community Garden is a
food oasis in Vancouver's Downtown Eastside.

Farm where you're planted, from frontyard blocks
to backyard beds to patio containers.

Close the
Loop:
Secret
Styrofoam

Amazingly, these
"stone" veggie
containers are
painted styrofoam
fish coolers!

Garden

Ward Teulon (wearing sunglasses) grew $28,000 worth of vegetables last year using neighborhood yards, boulevards and rooftops (cityfarmboy.com).

From farm to market to plate,
food is a beautiful thing.

Don't know where your food comes from?
Visit a pocket market, farmers' market or U-pick farm.

CERTIFIED ORGANIC
BUNCHED $2.50
CARROTS EACH

Cities and crops:
can't we all get along?

Garlic, onion and chives help deter pests and provide tasty results.

Choose fruit trees to
plant once and eat often.

June: corn, cucumbers, eggplant.

July: spinach, rutabaga.

August: onions, arugula, cauliflower, scallions, green manure
cover crops.

September: radishes, Oriental greens, salad blends.

October: garlic.

November: clean up and compost, rebuild structures.

December: sleep.

Rows or blocks?

Either method will work to grow crops. People who choose
blocks or sections say they use limited space more efficiently
and suppress weeds better (the chosen plants crowd out any unwanted guests that might deign to sprout). Some also say rows
are a vestige of industrial agriculture designed for big crews and
mechanical plows, so why bother? Then again, rows might have
an aesthetic appeal you like, and they do make it easy to get to
your crops.

Whichever you use it's worth creating spaces reserved only for
plants, not heavy-footed people. Sometimes people will double-
dig their blocks, a laborious way of deeply turning over soil to create a tall, loose, fluffy expanse of loam that will give roots plenty
of room to roam. Once created, you can never walk on top of this
area because you know this will only compact the soil beneath. If
you do go with blocks, make them no wider than an arm's length
from the sides so you can tend every part inside without having
to step in.

You can use almost anything to hold up the sides of your rows
or raised sections. The easiest way is to simply mound up the soil.
But you can go steeper and plant closer to the edges if you build
borders with stones, cinder blocks, tiles, pieces of hard plastic
held in place with stakes, or whatever else you find handy. If you go
with simple mounding, form shapes slightly wider at the base and
press lightly on the sides to firm the structure up before planting.

Weed creeps

Weeding is one of the least appealing jobs in farming, but you can't avoid it. Well, you can, but at your peril. Because the longer you wait, the stronger they get. Treat them as thieves who want to steal your vegetables' light and nutrients. If that doesn't work, extend the metaphor: the invaders are trying to take food off your plate! Hurry up! All hands to the fields! Pull the weeds up at once, or hoe them to death, and discard the remains (minus any seeds) in the compost. Repeat often.

Weed strategies get a lot of attention because weeds are everywhere. Some advise spraying vinegar or pouring boiling water on the invaders, or using tools of various odd configurations. Try everything or anything; I'm not sure you'll find any magic bullet beyond regular and diligent maintenance, and the earlier the better. Convince yourself you're tougher than the interlopers, and then have at them.

Walk This Way

Examples & Inspiration

Truck Farm is just what it says: a mobile community farm in the back of a 1986 Dodge. Started by filmmaker Ian Cheney (King Corn) because he wanted to grow food but didn't have anywhere to plant, it grew into a public art and environmental education campaign on wheels. Cheney and filmmaker partner Curt Ellis drove the truck to schools in eight states to show how creativity and urban agriculture can go together.

— truck-farm.com —

Water well

Unless you live in an area where the rain falls steadily and predict-ably throughout the growing season in precisely the proportions your plants require (also known as the Land of Dream-on), you're going to need to figure out irrigation.

A hose with a nozzle will be all the watering equipment most people with a small backyard section for food will ever need. You're doing the rest of the yard anyway, so the mini-farm won't add anything to your burden.

A drip irrigation system will appeal to those interested in con-serving our precious liquid resource (hose sprays and sprinklers can waste a lot in delivery). They can also be put on a timer for convenience or days you'll be away.

Rainwater harvesting

Another feature worth considering is rainwater harvesting. Al-ready becoming the norm in rain-challenged areas, this will grow in importance elsewhere as industrial farms draw down more of our natural aquifers. It isn't as pressing a concern where I live, but we may be getting there. Even in rainy Vancouver, the summers can stretch for weeks with no trace of moisture. Some of this is expected, but global climate weirdness could be making it worse. Our native red cedar, which has evolved to thrive in our climate, is now suffering in some places, perhaps from the greater intensity of these droughts.

Rainwater harvesting has probably been around as long as ag-riculture. Records show systems being used in India five thousand years ago. The world's largest cistern is the Yerebatan Sarayi in what is now Turkey. Built in 527 CE and capable of holding eighty thousand cubic meters of water in underground vaults, it's still a tourist attraction today.

The environmental nonprofit group GrowNYC has an excel-lent fifty-page color manual about rainwater harvesting available for free online. It explains how to choose and construct a system of your own. Even if you're not there yet, it's worth looking to get an idea of the size of the systems being built. People in Vancouver sometimes hear about rainwater harvesting, get enthused enough to set up a city-subsidized system in the shape of 55-gallon barrel that collects rain off a roof gutter, then believe they're doing a good thing for the Earth. And they are, but only 55 gallons worth. During the rainy months from early fall to late spring our regional reservoirs typically fill up, and the 55-gallon barrels stay filled as well (although your seedlings and indoor plants might appreciate a non-chlorinated drink). It's during the summers when we need the water that the barrels are most valuable, but once they're empty the owners are left looking up at the sky like everyone else. The answer, then, is bigger cisterns that can store more water when it falls in torrents. The rule of thumb for cistern costs is about $1 per gallon. Add another dollar per gallon to ship, and then more for plumbing and fixtures. The estimated cost in 2008 of a typical 1,000-gallon home system was $3,250, according to GrowNYC's Rainwater Harvesting 101 (grownyc.org/openspace /publications).

Root of the matter

When you do water, help your crops by watering deeply. Remember, you're watering the roots, not the leaves, even if you do think they must be terribly hot in that withering sun. Plants drink from the ground through their roots, so wetting their leaves may only encourage bacteria and fungi.

Deep watering once a week is usually enough for established plants (youngsters need it more often), but this depends on your local weather conditions and, of course, your soil. To find out whether you're watering enough, poke your finger into the soil. If it's moist down at root level, you're fine, but if it's dry, keep the water coming. In good loamy soil, according to researchers at Cornell University, 2.5 centimeters or 1 inch of water will penetrate to a depth of 38 centimeters (15 inches), which will do for most crops. An empty tuna can placed in the patch will fill up when you've added 2.5 centimeters of water.

The best time to water is in the early morning. Your plants will then be able to absorb and use the water for the long workday of photosynthesis ahead. If a plant's pipes run dry enough that its leaves wilt, not a rare sight, photosynthesis stops and won't be revived until a fresh drink perks everything up again.

Water in the evening if you must, but the earlier the better. Wet leaves at night can be host to mold and mildew and diseases, and cooling the soil with water while it's naturally losing heat anyway may delay germination or root growth in some plants. Also, an evening water that doesn't dry out before dark may keep wooden infrastructure such as planting box frames wet for a longer time, encouraging unwanted rot. You can also water in the middle of a hot day if that's all your schedule allows. It certainly feels better for the sweaty farmer. Garden books often disparage midday watering for how much gets wasted through evaporation, but I suspect this loss is more a function of the watering style than the time of day, and for small patches the difference doesn't add up to a lot anyway. Another non-starter is the guff I still see in books about the danger of a midday spray damaging leaves due to the scorching sun. I don't believe I've ever seen it happen. And if it did, wouldn't the tropics with their frequent cloudbursts be barren by now?

Class worms

The kids at Windemere High School mentioned in the aquaponics section above were also working on a worm compost system, which was amazing. Not the worms, although they were kind of incredible, but the fact that I went on a teachers' training day, which students across the province know as a vacation, yet here were several dozen digging their hands into the compost muck, tending the crops and fish in the courtyard greenhouse and building more vegetable beds for the organic farm taking over the school grounds. Nearby was an Earth Tub composter, a monster

Compost happens.

of a machine that can consume seventy kilos of food waste a day. To help feed it, the students were planning bicycle rides as part of a physical education course that would take them to other schools to pick up food waste. Anyone tempted to dismiss the youth of today as iPod-oblivious slackers should talk to some of the youth at Windemere.

Wriggling reds

Worms are foot soldiers in the new food revolution. With them you can eliminate the need to truck in costly fertilizers and truck out organic wastes. Worms will take that waste from you and turn it into some of the richest soil amendments you can find. Will Allen's farms at Growing Power are astounding for the amount of produce he coaxes from the soil. He doesn't bother thinning his spinach, for example, to let the individual plants grow to size. Instead he broadcast-seeds the pots or rows, lets everything come up, then harvests regularly with scissors-cuts, the spinach coming back up to nine times before it finally gives up. He gets away with such intense production methods thanks to his charges, millions of red wiggler worms (*Eisenia fetida*).

Allen's worm composting system starts with about a pound of worms on the bottom of a bin four by eight feet long and one foot deep. To that he adds two five-pound buckets of compost. Next comes a layer of worm food—you have to feed the troops or, as Napoleon put it, "An army marches on its stomach." This is where most people directly add food scraps, but Allen pre-digests the scraps first through composting. This speeds up

Will Allen from Growing Power checks his worm troops.

the worm's work and results in more uniform castings throughout the mix. On top of this goes a layer of finished castings and a burlap bag to keep the flies away and provide the darkness worms need. Check the bin for moisture (don't let it get too dry or too hot) and for food—if it's gone add another layer. You should see your worms get nice and fat and start to multiply (the cocoons look like little golden eggs).

Harvest the rich castings by placing window screening on top of the pile and laying food on it, topped with a layer of finished castings to deter flies. The worms will work their way through the tiny screen holes to reach the food over the next several days. Then dump the worms into a new bin and repeat the process. You can do this screen collecting three or four times, each time starting a new worm bin. Where are all these worms coming from? Themselves. They multiply four times in an eight-week period under this method. The finished castings can be dried and sifted through a wider screen to spread on the farm or be bagged to use later or sell.

Allen notes that anyone considering composting as a business should be aware that it is "very physical work that requires passion, patience, confidence and a strong work ethic plus consistency." He also recommends considering how much finished product you want to produce and how much material you'll need to get that amount. One ton of food waste produces approximately half a cubic yard of finished compost. Potential sources of organic waste materials include food banks (for spoiled produce), restaurants, local farmers, local breweries (for the spent grain, not the free samples), grocery stores, coffee shops and city grounds crews that often have huge piles of leaves, wood chips and grass clippings.

Global grower

The Union of Concerned Scientists want you to know that as a grower you have a role to play in saving the planet by combating global warming. Want to be part of the solution? The following steps are based on their suggestions.

Five ways to practice Earth-friendly farming

1. Minimize carbon-emitting inputs to your operation. Say no to the gas-powered mower and leaf-blower, ditch the synthetic fertilizers and pesticides. Roundup, the Monsanto herbicide, is singled out for mention by the scientists as one of the most carbon-emitting pesticides available. Just sayin'.
2. Don't leave soil bare. That makes it vulnerable not only to erosion and weeds but to carbon loss as well. Plant cover crops which increase fertility, reducing the need for energy-intensive fertilizers.
3. Plant trees and shrubs. They remove heat-trapping CO_2 from the atmosphere every year as they mature. The urban trees of the contiguous United States accumulate 23 million tons of carbon every year, more than all the homes, cars and industries emit in Los Angeles County.
4. Recycle by composting. Backyard operations are good, and so are citywide efforts such as the mandatory recycling program in San Francisco where residents have blue, green

and black bins for recyclables, compost and trash. The city collects more than four hundred tons of food scraps and other compostables every day.

5. Reconsider that lawn. About 80 percent of all US householders have access to a private lawn. It will be a grand day when all of them follow Michelle Obama's lead and tear up at least part of their turf to grow organic food.

TAKE HOME MESSAGE

Food is beautiful, from seed to plate.

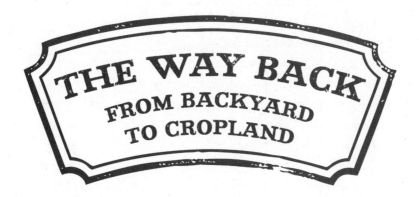

CHAPTER 4

THE WAY BACK
FROM BACKYARD TO CROPLAND

That last chapter? Amusing, perhaps, but really, we're talking about the future of the world here. Or at least the future of your pantry. Those onions were fine, they went great with the broccoli tips, but that's hardly slaked your appetite. You are ready to get serious now. You want to fill up on this stuff, keep the family fed, maybe even grow a surplus. Honey, we're redoing the backyard. Yes. The whole backyard.

If this seems audacious, because a backyard is supposed to include a lawn and a barbecue and a tool shed and games, consider that devoting your entire backyard to food makes more sense than some recreational ruse you hardly ever pursue anyway (when was the last time you took that croquet set out of the garage?).

Some immigrants, feeling less constrained by North American convention to view their lawns as social weapons, caught on as soon as they got here and turned their backyards into food production facilities. You can see them if you walk the lanes and peer over fences, the Chinese using pallets as trellises to hold up squash, the Italians with hockey stick handles as stakes for tomatoes and bell peppers, Russians tending rows of potatoes and beets and Latinos crowding the space with corn and squash and beans.

The concept of the yard itself is of course different in each of the countries these neighbors come from. In Japan, where I used to live, urban agriculture is the norm even in the most tightly packed residential areas. You see the most unlikely juxtapositions, rows of homes suddenly giving way to a lot devoted to daikon radishes, or a rice paddy, or a mini-orchard. This could be attributed to the agrarian roots of Japanese culture which survive urbanization because they've been nurtured by habit and policy — property owners can save a bundle on their taxes if they use these spaces to grow food.

Turning your backyard into a mini-farm is really just an extension of the vegetable patch we discussed already. Instead of adding crops in and among the flowers and things, you can transform your entire yard into a dedicated vegetable growing space. When you look upon your domain and see that it's all about the food, you know you're getting serious. This marks an important passage because it takes you away from the realm of the mainstream lawn-slave and into the cutting edge of urban agriculture. You are rejecting the expected use of your space and replacing it with a more enlightened view of what city land can be. If you harbor any lingering concerns about what you may be giving up in aesthetics, don't worry. A property bulging from fence to fence with crops can be an inspiring sight, and one you'll be eager to show off.

FOUR REASONS TO CONVERT YOUR BACKYARD TO CROPS

1. Scaled-up production creates a surplus you can share/sell/preserve.
2. Increases time spent outdoors in healthy activity.
3. No more mowing, spraying, feeding, dosing your turf.
4. Enhances biodiversity and reduces greenhouse gases.

Food all the way to the fence.

What to grow?

You have the same choices described in previous chapters, but the added space gives you many more options in variety and quantity. An entire backyard reserved for food means you'll need to be strategic with your annual plan, staggering crop selections and planting times so you don't get a huge harvest followed by all that fallow space to look at until next spring.

If a bigger spread seems daunting in terms of the time commitment, consider how much of the space you might plant in perennials, which have the advantage of coming back year after year without your help. Depending on your climate, you might try asparagus, artichokes, kale, rhubarb, strawberries or fruiting shrubs.

Some herbs are tough enough to overwinter or self-seed to appear again next spring. Consider arugula, ordinary and garlic chives, thyme, oregano and lovage.

Flowers that can also become a recurring theme include daylilies, alliums, borage, nasturtium and marigolds.

Design matters

Your decision to grow crops for the whole backyard creates new opportunities for your design. A mini-farm can take on any of a variety of shapes that will affect how much you enjoy looking at your space — and how well it functions for you. So before you start digging, it's a good idea to sit down and decide just what you want. Or you can design the way many people do, with a shovel, working it out as you go along. It's not necessarily a bad plan, but your chances of getting what you want rise considerably if you spend a little time working things out before wading in.

Start by asking yourself some basic questions. Do you prefer a look that's more formal (straight rows) or funky (beds amongst curvy paths)? Straight rows are a recognizable theme in agriculture, which you may or may not prefer, while a looser look might involve a winding path that leads to sections of food growing on both sides.

Don't ask, don't till

Or for a truly natural approach you might consider "no-till" growing. The idea, as Japanese farmer Masanobu Fukuoka explains in *One Straw Revolution*, is that "the earth cultivates itself." He believed it was wrong for humans to try to do what roots and worms and microorganisms do better. Plowing the soil only turns up weed seeds and gives them the opportunity to grow (something any farmer will attest to in spring). Better, said Fukuoka, to go natural, adding fertility and out-competing the weeds with beneficial cover crops and timely planting of your desired varieties of food.

To follow nature, work in layers: fruit trees above, grains or taller vegetables next, ground cover under that and root vegetables below ground. You'll get similar ideas by looking into the practice of "permaculture," which is just another way of saying natural farming or growing food ecologically. Take all these examples and come up with what works best for you and your particular land.

Fukuoka himself was a bit of an eccentric (he tried to talk the Rodale folks out of promoting composting), but his own small farm on the island of Shikoku became a global standard-bearer in alternative agriculture, a healthy antidote when the rest of Japan was turning to chemical-soaked industrial farms. He died in 2008 at the age of ninety-five, but his life remains a testament to the powers of observation. His whole philosophy is based on what he learned watching nature at work on his own trees and crops. Your backyard should be no less instructive.

Ten characteristics of good design

Like art, people often know what they like even if they lack the words to articulate it. Create your backyard farm so that it will be:

- Holistic (the parts and the whole complement each other)
- Harmonious with its surroundings
- Respectful of systems, flows, patterns
- The right size
- Simple
- Efficient
- Resilient
- Biodiverse
- Natural
- Beautiful

Bad design is, well, look around. Our lives are cluttered with it. Cheap building materials thrown together with little care for anything beyond profit, public benches almost cruelly unsuited for the human spine, shrubs tortured into freakish shapes, roads that take you in circles away from your desired destination, cities clogged with cars because human connections were ignored, failed states and on and on. But let's not dwell. Let's design.

While it's not strictly necessary, it can prove useful to keep your drawing to scale. This will help the further you get into the process by making it easier to see at a glance why that sketched bench might prove to be a little long at eighty feet.

A 1:100 scale will probably fit a concept design of your backyard onto a single page with room for labels and comments, although

1:50 might make things easier to visualize. A more detailed plan within that space for a particular patch or something like a bench could be 1:20 or 1:10. These ratios describe the difference in size between what you draw on your paper (the first number) and the actual thing (the second number). So a centimeter on your paper, at 1:100, would equal 100 centimeters, or one meter, in the yard. A triangular scale rule — available at many office supply stores or anywhere that sells drafting goods — makes it easy to size things at once, or you can use graphed paper and count the squares.

Once you draw a base outline of your backyard, including the house, paths, garage, trees and so on, tape a piece of tracing paper over it and begin sketching out ideas. Tracing paper isn't so expensive that you shouldn't feel free to draw wildly, ripping up and replacing the paper with each newer and better scheme. You can also design with a computer, using a simple and free software such as SketchUp which lets you pull your 2D flat images up into 3D shapes.

Whether done on paper or screen, the design process can be enjoyable, a happy indoor pursuit to get lost in, but it's also good to keep going outside to "ground truth" your design. Use props as spatial keys to help you see just what you're thinking. Take-out chopsticks and string or flagging tape can mark out planting beds; bamboo poles can stand in for fruit trees; two chairs and a plank can serve as a bench. Try switching things around to judge how different placements affect the look from different areas, including inside the house.

There are any number of ways to start drawing out your design ideas. Try different approaches to see which work for you. Scribble happily until you see something start to emerge from the mess; use geometric shapes such as circles, triangles and rectangles to see how the overlaps might begin to suggest a theme; sketch on a grid and then tilt the whole thing at an angle to see what develops. Use whatever works best to open your creative spigot, then let it flow. You may be delighted to see how quickly the trickle becomes a gush.

Paths

Some prefer to begin with an ordering device such as circulation, a crucial aspect since whatever design you end up with must allow you to move into and through the site, perhaps while carrying heavy bags or tools. And no matter what you're growing, you'll need direct access to the planting areas so you can tend to the crops, eliminate weeds and harvest the results.

Paths can be laid straight in a grid pattern or curved in a more serendipitous-like web. Growers are sometimes tempted to minimize the width of paths to fit more food, because isn't that the whole point? Yes, but go too narrow and it'll make moving around your farm unpleasant. Pathways between rows can be as narrow as 30 centimeters (12 inches) but anything slimmer than that will have you placing your steps carefully, which means slowly. For the main pathways you may want to allow at least 70 centimeters (27 inches) to make moving about easy even when using bulky items like wheelbarrows.

If you're in an area where the growing season is not also the monsoon, you may get away with leaving the paths as bare soil. But depending on your site's drainage, this strategy could turn your walkways into a mud zone that you'd be reluctant to travel on without boots. To get above the muck, cover your paths with straw or hay, sand, bark chips, old bricks, pea gravel, road base, gravel, used blocks of sidewalk, wooden planks, concrete pavers or whatever else you might have on hand. If you're using bark chips a 5-centimeter (2-inch) layer will last about two years and a 7.5-centimeter (3-inch) layer about three years — although different types and sizes of bark and local conditions can alter that time. Some of these materials may make your resident slug population very happy. Others, such as the gravel, should be laid thickly enough to avoid being scuffed aside into bare patches: about 4 centimeters (1¼ inches) will work, although double that amount will last longer. You'll also want to keep a loose material like gravel in place with borders made of wood, brick or stone. This means more work for you in the beginning, but less maintenance later on.

You can save yourself a lot of weeding work later by first laying under your path landscaping cloth, such as geotextile polypropylene, before you add the covering material. For a brick or stone path, add a 5-centimeter (2 inch) base of compacted sand (you can rent a compactor at the tool rental store). Then fix the bricks or stones in place, brushing cement or mortar into the spaces for added stability. A level will help you keep the path flat, but not perfectly flat: include a slight slope so that water will run off in the direction you choose, while avoiding pockets or depressions where it might pool.

Borders and fences

A fence can protect your garden — deer love salad greens even more than your vegan friends do — or help define and separate its uses. The choices are many. A single strand of electrified wire strung between dug-in posts can deter some critters, while you will probably need a double-layered anti-deer netting fence to keep Bambi's family at bay if you live in their world. The aesthetic choices run from quaint white picket to cedar split rail to institutional chain link.

Living fences are another possibility. Willow branches placed with both ends in the ground to form arcs will grow wherever they're planted. Willow contains a hormone that spurs root growth (this is a good thing to keep in mind when propagating other plants: soak some cut willow branches in a bucket of water overnight and then dip the rooting side of the plants you're trying to grow into the water before planting). Willow fences will sprout green in summers, which can be attractive. They will also try to throw up more branches to turn back into trees, but you can easily snip off the upright shoots to maintain the arcs as an attractive and free natural border.

Ins and outs

Think about how people will enter and leave your backyard farm. This should be considered together with the circulation, particularly if you expect visitors. Their first and often most lasting impression will be formed by how they approach and enter the site. This can be important for you as well. A wide, inviting entrance may lure you into the farm area more often.

A gate says a lot, so put some thought into what you use. It can be wood, or iron, or recycled materials, or whatever. It can be easy and inviting to use, a simple push on a swinging door, or more troublesome, a high-latch affair to keep small children at bay.

Benches and sheds

A bench placed in a prominent place amid your growing empire can be an attraction you will visit often to sit, record your exploits in a planting log or just relax with a frosty beverage to replace

A tool shed can also be a focal point.

the fluids lost in hard farm labor. Apply the same thinking to the placement of a shed. It may be the kind of thing you tuck into a far corner so it's out of the way, but could also be a central attraction, something seen as an essential part of a working farm. You could even make it nice enough inside, with a mini-bench and fold-down table, to spend time in.

Design flexibility

You can construct paths and planting areas that will not change once you've laid them out, or design adaptability into your farm from the start by creating paths that you don't expect to last more than a year or two. The former will make it easier to build up fluffy, untrampled soil over the years, but the latter will permit design tinkerers to think anew with each growing season, perhaps trying vastly different layouts until they find one that can no longer be improved upon because it's perfect.

No matter which method you choose, plan on rotating your crops. The danger with growing potatoes or tomatoes or garlic in the same spots every year is that pathogens are likely to catch up. This year my garlic, for instance, finally got hit with rust, a fungus which overwinters in the soil, because I grew it continually in the same patch. Also, plants which use more of a certain trace mineral than another will have less chance to deplete an area if you rotate. Moving your crops around each year before they can develop problems is a good precautionary strategy.

Hoop house how-to

A hoop house is a relatively accessible way to build an unheated greenhouse without going to all the expense and effort of building an actual greenhouse. Although there still is some expense and effort involved in a model using curved PVC pipe and plastic sheeting, and it won't hold up as long as a more formidable structure, you'll get the same benefits in extending your farming options to every month of the year.

Hoop houses can offer high value at low cost.

The Kerr Center for Sustainable Agriculture out of Oklahoma offers a pdf with step-by-step instructions and photos on building a low-cost hoop house. The pictures may suggest you need a small army to put the contraption up, but fear not: the crowd is part of a workshop learning the technique. (kerrcenter.com/publications /hoophouse/index.htm)

Two-block diet

Kate Sutherland didn't have the land she needed to grow the vegetables she wanted in her Vancouver neighborhood. But she found a neighbor who did, and who also shared her passion for growing more local food as an alternative to industrial agriculture.

They suspected they weren't alone, so they handed out leaflets around the block. Thirteen people showed up to the first meeting, and the Two-Block Diet became a movement.

The group now shares a collection of backyards they tend together, all showing up at one place for work parties to do group tasks such as assembling a plastic greenhouse or setting up a new beehive. The mutual support network goes beyond farming.

When one of the member's husbands got sick, the others took turns bringing meals for the couple.

Their blog (twoblockdiet.blogspot.com/) includes a link to *Two Block Diet — An Unmanual.* They recommend first connecting with one to three friends, and if all agree, taking the idea of a food-growing group to others on the same street. Then it's time to call a meeting, for which they have the following advice.

- Meet at a time that is the most convenient for the majority (Sunday afternoon works best for us).
- Start on time and end on time. People are generally more comfortable committing to share their time if it is respected.
- Meet once every two weeks in the off-season (winter) and start taking action as soon as you can. People can easily get "meeting burnout."
- Take notes at the meeting and email them to everyone or post them on a website or blog.
- If people commit to actions at a meeting ("I'll call my friend so and so to see if she'll donate some manure") make sure to follow up. It helps facilitate consistency and respect. We often start our meetings with a check-in from each person to report on what they've done since the last meeting.
- See if you can recruit an experienced gardener. It is great if you have someone who can share knowledge, or talk down a panicked tomato lover who has discovered a spot.
- Once we had settled on a time and day that worked well for everyone, we decided to get cracking on work parties. The idea is that each week we go to one person's garden to tackle a large project that would take a single person at least a day or two to do themselves. The results have been quite dramatic, visually and emotionally. We have all learned to value the experience of giving, but most importantly, we all take a turn on the receiving end, which helps immensely when it comes to seeing ourselves as valuable people within our community.

- We operate under the idea that we already have everything we need right here. Your neighbourhood is full of free resources like leaves, compost, sticks, boards, bricks, pipes, cardboard, boxes, abandoned shelves and amazing things that can be converted into planters.
- A big part of this project for some of us is helping other neighborhoods to start and maintain projects like these because we've all been blown away by how simple, effective and fulfilling this has been. We can't imagine going back to the way things were before our mini garden revolution. Funny that talking to your neighbors has become an act of rebellion. So, if you want help organizing something like this in your neighborhood, just ask.

Borrowed land farmer — Arzeena Hamir

Arzeena Hamir is a professional agronomist and agrologist who coordinates the Richmond Food Security Society next to Vancouver. Three years ago Hamir and two friends decided to add to their already busy lives by grow-ing food commercially, using other people's yards. This is an increasingly popular idea in urban agriculture in some parts of the world, where property owners may be intrigued by the idea of offering their land for free. Sometimes there's a payoff in a share of the harvest, but often not. Anyone wondering about the economics of growing and selling city food on bor-rowed land might find something of value in Hamir's experience.

Her Richmond Urban Farmers group began by putting a small notice in a local paper. A single homeowner

Arzeena Hamir.

responded to offer a 400-square-foot yard. Hamir says they jumped on it without giving much thought to what it might cost to convert the area into a farm.

"We spent, I don't know, $400 converting their front garden. We rented rototillers, we got sod-cutters, we brought in probably 10 yards of compost. It was like the Cadillac garden, and darned if that thing was not going to grow *something*. We ended up planting four mounded beds."

Once the food grew they realized they hadn't thought about how to market it, so Hamir sent an email to friends. Enough replied to her offer of $10 baskets of local organic vegetables to make it worth the effort, so the following spring they added a larger borrowed space. This one was a 2,000-square-foot backyard formerly tended by an avid gardener who had passed away. His widow heard about the Richmond Urban Farmers and thought they might make better use of it.

"We spent two days just pulling weeds. But under the weeds was rich dark soil that had been gardened for two decades and was beautiful. We also got to use her shed so that we could leave tools. I think we brought in one load of manure. Things grew really well. So that was the year that we decided to formalize by starting a mailing list and selling shares, although I think we were still only selling them for $15 a share."

Food left after the share division was sold once a month at a pocket farmers' market in Vancouver. Some of the greens they put on sale surprised even the other farmers.

"We sold a lot of weeds. Our first salad mix was chickweed, purslane and sorrel. We added some more vegetables to high-end $7 bags. We also did a deal where we stuffed a ziplock bag with chickweed, added a bunch of carrots and radishes, and sold it for, I can't remember, $10 or something. We gave out samples, and they just flew. A lot of people hadn't eaten chickweed before and thought it was cool. We estimated we sold chickweed for $15 a pound."

Success from the shares and the Vancouver market meant they were able to pay off their debt from the first year on the Cadillac garden, as well as what they had invested in the second garden. Then they added another yard, but this time they didn't want to spend money converting it to cropland. So they went with sheet mulching, which sounded as if it was going to be easy.

"It was 500 square feet. We just figured, we'll sheet mulch it, sure. Do you have any *idea* how much cardboard that is? Five hundred square feet is a ton of cardboard. We thought, all right, we'll go to Trail Appliance, we'll get all their fridge boxes. Well, you put a fridge on the ground it's like five square feet. It's not that big. So we finally found a source of cardboard, the local newspaper. Between their bundles of paper they have this much thinner cardboard and it's round circles. All free."

Still looking to save investment costs on nutrients, they decided to pick up seaweed, also for free, from nearby Boundary Bay. Seaweed turns out to be heavier than it looks.

"When it's dry, you can fill a bag and balance it in your hand. When it's wet? Oh my god, we killed ourselves hauling this stuff. It almost broke the axel on the truck. Also, when it's wet it doesn't spread. You couldn't lift half a garbage bag. Then you dump it, and because it's all wet and matting you can't spread it. Honestly, fifty bags of seaweed. *Now* it's funny, but not then."

To add to the seaweed, Hamir's group opted for the city's composted yard trimmings waste, a decent soil amendment sold for a nominal $5 per small truckload. But it was another surprise to learn how many trips to the landfill and how much wheelbarrowing this involved. Eventually the third yard was set up too, at very little cost, but huge time and effort. So when a fourth yard option came up, they decided to do a hybrid. They went with sheet mulching again, but rather than slog out multiple trips to the beach and the landfill, they just ordered a load of mushroom manure from a local garden soil delivery company. It cost more, but could be dumped on top of their cardboard and planted in immediately. So now the Richmond Urban Farmers had a farm spread over four sites, which wasn't a bad thing since the different conditions supported different crops. Potatoes are a struggle for one site that has wire worm but do well at another, while the first area is good for lettuce.

Judge for yourself whether the economics add up. To help work the numbers, one of Hamir's partners bought the SPIN manual. SPIN stands for Small Plot INtensive growing, as described by Saskatchewan farmer Wally Satzewich, who says you can gross $50,000 worth of crops on half an acre. Hamir's group was a fair piece short of that, but she remains supportive of the concept.

"They concentrate on the high-value crops that are very short season. I don't know why Saskatoon has this huge market for radishes but Wally makes $400 a week selling them when we couldn't give them away. At the end of the year we calculated we made about $1.50 a square foot, whereas SPIN farming is a $3-a-square-foot operation. You would be busting your ass making $3 a square foot. For us, all three of us have other jobs. None of us wanted to make the commitment of jumping into this full-time. SPIN is primarily selling through farmers' markets where you get the best price for your produce. In Vancouver it would probably have to be in [pricey] Kits or the West End where they can charge a lot. We wouldn't be able to charge that amount here in Richmond. The other thing that makes it easier is they bundle, like, five beets, and charge by the piece rather than by weight. I'm not going to shell out $300 for a commercial scale. It's sold in either $1.50 or $3 bundles that anyone can look at and understand. But going to farmers' markets — holy smokes. Not only are you there all day, usually, but it's also taken you a day to prep, so it's a two-day commitment for each market you go to. I think Wally goes to three markets a week to make his $3 a square foot.

"The other thing you need with SPIN farming is a cooler. He recommends an adapter you can get that adapts an air conditioner into a cooler. Supposedly it works. That's so you can harvest slowly over the week. In our case we would harvest some vegetables at 7 PM. For other ones like squash flowers and lettuce we would be up at 5 AM with headlamps, harvesting in the dark. That was last year and I'm like, I am *not* doing this again unless I'm getting paid more money."

Heads you win.

Is it paydirt?

"We'll get an average $140 a week from our $20 boxes. And for that I would say, Susan and Luc are here for a couple of hours on Wednesday, so four hours total for them, and I do maybe three hours on Thursdays. I deliver or people pick up at my place. So seven hours total, once everything is planted, is doable. We're all enjoying it now; it's not stressful. If we were trying to pump 15 shares out of this place every week it would be different. If you do that, you're constantly replanting. So this is the hybrid, kind of the urbanite's way of farming. You still get an income that isn't bad, it pays for me to buy a whole bunch of organic peaches and tomatoes to can, and it pays for some extra stuff. Also you eat well, because you pick extra and eat the stuff like forked carrots and things that break."

Will she do it again next year?

"We're talking about it already."

Natural pest appeasement

It's bound to happen. Your blue-sky ideal of Eden with bountiful crops is suddenly clouded by an invading army. Big surprise: by laying out a sumptuous, all-you-can buffet, bugs have noticed, and started showing up in droves. What do you do?

First what you don't do. Don't freak out. Don't reach for the poison. Don't destroy the village in order to save it.

Organic means we understand we're tending an ecosystem, remember? We're working with nature on this campaign. But that doesn't mean we have to sit back and watch things eat our lunch. When you with work with nature, you still get to tweak it to make sure it works the way you choose.

Here's one strategy for the lazy among us (don't raise your hand, just nod gently): do nothing. Or almost nothing. From *Shepherd's Purse: Organic Pest Control Handbook*:

> "Some preventative measures, cultural and biological, are necessary but to our surprise and pleasure we have found that doing nothing or very little in the way of insect control turns out to be not only the safest way to garden but usually the best and most effective insect control around. Every now and then pest populations can get out of balance and we have to do something about the bugs, but that happens far less than we ever could have imagined when we first began gardening."

Integrated pest massacre

There's another approach that involves more effort all around. It's not organic but lays claims to common sense. Integrated Pest Management or IPM encourages growers to understand insects,

monitor their plants for insect populations, determine the level of plant injury and — in the rare event that a population is found to be above the threshold of tolerance — use control strategies which may include natural enemies, cultural controls and, wait for it, selected pesticides. Meaning: you still get to nuke the vermin. But in a thoughtful way.

I was more interested in IPM before I visited a U-pick strawberry farm

Bugs aren't all bad.

where it was touted. With no organic strawberry options nearby, and posters describing how the spraying option was such a tiny part of the farm's comprehensive IPM system, it seemed acceptable. During a break from the berry picking, I spotted some duckweed floating beside the crops in a drainage ditch. We had an outdoor fountain with a few plants and goldfish on our balcony that I thought would look good with duckweed, so I scooped a few cupfuls into a jar and took it home. A day later the goldfish were dead. And these were fish that had lived through all manner of harsh conditions including neglect for two years. Maybe it was a coincidence, maybe it was one of the pesticides that's said to be harmless to people but lethal to fish, or maybe there was no connection to the ditch water and whatever runoff it might have held. I still think IPM seems like a sound idea. But I get my strawberries from another farm.

Squeeze play

Rather than shopping for something toxic, your first instinct, if it's to squash the dastardly interlopers, is probably the best. Physical controls are often the first choice of the environmentally engaged farmer. Start early enough, before an infestation of caterpillars, slugs or snails takes hold, and you may be able to stay ahead of them. Let them know you mean business by squeezing all you can catch between your fingertips (the squeamish may wear gloves) or by dropping them into a can of soapy water, or, easier still, squashing them under the sole of your boot.

You can also try a hand-held vacuum to suck bugs up and out of mind—borrowing a strategy from commercial strawberry growers in California who use tractor-mounted vacuums to eliminate the problem. Another technique professionals monitoring for bugs use is to place a drop cloth beneath a plant or tree and shake the leaves. Early mornings tend to be best, when the bugs are still cool and slow. Those that land on the sheet can be marched off to the drowning barrel or the garbage. You won't get all the intruders, but maybe enough to stem the invasion. Other physical control measures include keeping the pests from reaching your plants with protective mulch or a band of diatomaceous earth (crushed exoskeletons and remains of tiny marine animals) spread onto the soil. Winged critters can be kept away by draping a floating row cover over the plants.

Bio-weapons

Biological controls require a little study to match the pest with the appropriate natural enemy. Living organisms that can serve as your mercenaries include beneficial predators which you attract by planting the flowers and habitat-friendly plants they desire, and store-bought choices such as ladybugs and the soil-living bacterium Bt (*Bacillus thuringiensis*).

Chemical friends

Chemical controls you can use and still consider yourself organic include some commercially-made insecticidal soaps; neem oil spray; and a concoction you can make yourself by soaking a clove of crushed garlic and a diced hot pepper in water overnight, then straining to remove the solids and pouring into a spray bottle. Spray often; bugs that have yet to develop an appreciation for Szechuan cuisine are supposed to stay away as long as you keep the scent on leaves.

Slug fest

West coast farmers are accustomed to doing battle with slugs and aphids. Slugs can be picked (use an old pair of old cooking chopsticks if you're sensitive to slime), then squashed underfoot, dropped into a tin filled with salty water or flung into your neighbor's yard. The best slug-hunting time is in the late evening or early morning when they come out to feed. The most dedicated wear headlamps for night patrols. You can also try drowning slugs in a shallow dish of beer, unless it offends your common sense to stand drinks to ingrates. Some farmers swear by traps, placing a wooden plank or half of an upside-down orange amid their crops, then simply turning these over in the early morning to find the slugs.

Blasted aphids

Aphids are best knocked off leaves with a strong blast of water. They can't just dry out and come back; they are sucking insects that hold on with their mouths, so the forced eviction renders them useless. Intervene early and often to stay ahead of the trend. On new apple leaves, for instance, if you wait too long they will extract enough liquid to be able to hunker down inside the curled leaves. You can still get at them, unfurling the leaves one by one, but it's bothersome. If you see ants crawling up and down the trunk of your aphid-ridden tree, it's not a coincidence. The ants are farming too. They bring aphids up to the tender new leaves, wait for them to extract the sap, then milk the aphids for the honeydew. Fascinating, yes, but no help to us. Blast the ants as well as the aphids out of the tree, then wind a six-inch band of plastic wrap around the trunk and coat it with something super-sticky like Tree Tanglefoot. One application should be enough to block the route to work for ants for an entire season.

Bug farmer — Maria Keating

Maria Keating is the self-described "Bug Lady" at the City Farmer organic garden demonstration site in Vancouver. She also works as a biological control consultant to the greenhouse industry. She's gotten to know bugs well over the past fifteen years, enough to like them, and in her infectious enthusiasm there may

Maria Keating.

be some points for others to consider. Most people are so put off they recoil at the very idea of bugs. But if you're going to work with nature to control pests, Keating says, you have to start paying attention to the natural world that is your farm.

"What I tell people is not all bugs are bad and evil. When you start to learn about them and their habitats you find they're really very interesting and they all have their own stories. If you just overturn a leaf and look, there's so much there."

Interesting or otherwise, they're definitely useful, in ways many people are unaware.

"It's not just ladybugs. I could tell you a good twenty aphid predators. If you can appreciate bugs you're going to be a better gardener. You're going to let things grow to see what happens, and learn from it. Those are the surprises when you start gardening and bringing those green spaces into the cities. I tell kids who visit here it's like a fairy garden: if you don't believe in it you're never going to see it."

Does organic farming work from a pest control perspective?

"That's always the big question with organic gardening: does it work? People never question pesticides, but you know what? Pesticides have resistance, and pesticides have side effects. In university my first job was with Health Canada doing a pesticide exposure study with farmers in Ontario, and it blew me away. I had to go to talk to families about the pesticides they were spraying like 2,4-D, and the exposure to the farmer, typically to his wife and a child, too. It was really crazy. I thought they were going to view me as this government person trying to tell them stuff but instead it was them telling me about cancers in their families and how they didn't want to go there. It was totally different from what I expected."

Tool talk — Bob Denman

Of course you know quality tools and proper tool care are important, as all the books say. Yet you can't resist the temptation to buy the $9.99 shovel because, hell, it's only $9.99.

I know how it goes. I'm cheap too. But I think I can change. To help get me there, I asked Bob Denman for advice. Denman owns Red Pig Tools, selling high-quality, handmade pieces of outdoor art that are built to do the job properly and last a long time (Red pigtools.com). His product list has two thousand different kinds of tools, including more than two hundred he crafts himself. He also invents tools, custom-makes tools for people who know what they want but have never seen it on a store shelf, and lectures about proper tool selection and use.

I started by offering my theory that the typical urban farmer doesn't know much about tools. He agreed.

"Most people don't know what tools to use and even common ones they don't use really well. Hand them a shovel and they'll dig poorly. They end up sore and tired, unnecessarily. I see people who earn a living digging poorly. A lot of people have worked this way all their life because nobody ever told them how to dig properly."

How to dig a hole

Denman offered an explanation of some things you might have thought you knew well, including how to dig.

1. Dig when your soil is wet. It should be the consistency of a wrung-out sponge. If not, water it.
2. Choose the right tool. The most common kind found in garages in North America is the round-point shovel, also known as an American pattern, which should be fine. Use the long-handled type that's appropriate to your height. The D-handle ones may look handier but are actually harder on your back.
3. Make sure your shovel is sharp. Manufacturers assume buyers know they're supposed to sharpen the blade, but a surprising number of buyers don't, and dig with a dull shovel for the rest of their lives. Use a file such as a draw file at an angle of 30–45 degrees, creating an edge that should be sharp enough to cut you. Keep it sharp with occasional passes with

the file while you're in the field, like a butcher who knows it's easier to keep a blade honed than to sharpen a dull one.

4. Dig with the blade close to your foot. Place the blade in the soil in front of your toe, then step on it to drive it straight down with your body weight. When you pull back, if you have the right lift (blade angle) in your shovel, your back will stay straight. Then squat, sliding your lower hand down to lift with your legs rather than with your back. Toss the soil in a way that doesn't twist your back under the load.

5. Don't take too big a bite. Hauling up a huge clump of soil and then slicing or beating it into smaller pieces is a waste of effort. Taking up smaller chunks is more efficient and easier on the body.

6. If you're digging a trench for a vegetable bed, take thin spits (spadefuls of soil). Dig the opening, then work across it by adding two inches at a time. Because the trench is negative space in front of you, and you're only taking two inches, it's easy to drive the blade in — the dirt displaces slightly forward. Instead of coming back ten inches and fighting the entire resistance and inertia of a large clump, a thin spit comes up easily. Pull back and flick the soil to the far side of the trench. Because it is a thin, unstable plane, it will shatter, unlike a great unstable mass that you have to slice through and flatten with the shovel.

I also asked for recommendations on a basic tool kit that would get an urban farmer going. Denman had to think for a moment — "there are an awful lot of tools" — before suggesting the following.

Six tools to get started

1. A long-handled, round-point shovel to pick up and move dirt.
2. A spade for digging beds, the straight face and rectangular bottom of the blade helping to make beds of a uniform depth.

3. A spading fork as an alternative to a digging spade or shovel for heavy ground with a lot of clay, because there's less friction on the tines than on a flat face.

4. A cultivator with one to four tines for working in soil amendments and to keep moisture in the soil. (Tilling breaks up the soil, creating air pockets that any water wicking up will go to. If those air pockets aren't there, as in a clay soil where the particles are crammed close together, the water wicks up quicker, which is why you see that crusty surface develop in dry weather.)

5. A heavy rake to level new beds. Light ones may seem easier but are actually more work since you have to apply pressure with each draw. A heavy rake need only be thrown and then pulled back so its own weight gathers the soil.

6. A hoe to get rid of weeds. They come with blades in all shapes and angles and sizes. The ones with blades almost parallel to the ground are good at slicing weeds, while the ones with upright blades are better at pushing and pulling soil. Pick one that suits your purpose and that you happen to like.

Finally I asked Denman about proper care for tools, another skill where I suspect many urban farmers are lacking.

He explained that tools with fiberglass handles, which he doesn't recommend, can be cleaned off with soap and water, and occasionally with acetone. All wood handle tools, from small hand tools up to long-handled rakes or hoes, should be inspected once or twice a year. If the grain is starting to open, sand them lightly. There's no need to varnish the handles. Instead get boiled linseed oil from the hardware store or paint store, thinning it with a little penetrating turpentine if the tool is really old and dried out, and slop it on. Then go away. Come back in fifteen minutes. If the oil is soaked in, do it again. Repeat the process until you come back and find the soil still standing on the surface. Then take a dry cloth and buff it off.

The metal parts should be cleaned off with a wire brush. Once a year, say in fall when the tool is likely to be put up for a few months, coat it with oil to prevent rust. Used motor oil poured onto a rag will do. Some people keep an old barrel filled with coarse sand into which they pour a couple of gallons of used motor oil. At the end of the day simply jam your tools into the barrel and they'll be perfectly oiled. But don't do this with your hand pruners—grit can get between the blades and eventually loosen them.

I ended by asking why anyone should spend money on an expensive tool when there are so many cheaper options in the stores.

"You should buy the best tool you can afford. Cheap tools don't work as well and they break easily, especially when you're doing some kind of agriculture. In the class I teach I keep some heads of cheap tools that are practically a compendium of how they break. The cheaper the tool, the thinner the walls are going to be.

Walk This Way

Examples & Inspiration

On the shoreline of the East River and with a sweeping view of the Manhattan skyline, Eagle Street Rooftop Farm is a 6,000-square-foot green-roof organic vegetable farm located atop a warehouse rooftop in Greenpoint, Brooklyn. During New York City's growing season, the farmers at Eagle Street Rooftop Farm supply a community supported agriculture (CSA) program, an onsite farm market, and bicycle fresh produce to area restaurants.

— rooftopfarms.org —

"Cheap handles will also fail on you. They have to use low-grade instead of high-grade wood. Tool handles come in about six or seven different grades from lowest to highest. The tight-grain, knot-free, really good ones are more expensive.

"If you buy a really good, high-quality tool with a good handle on it, it's going to last year after year after year. A good forged shovel, which is about $90 nowadays depending on where you buy it and what model you get, can last through three or four generations of people before it finally gets worn out. If you buy the $9.99 tool, you're probably going to buy one every season or so, and maybe even several in a season.

"It's true with any type of tool. Buy the best tool you can afford because it's going to last longer. It's also going to work right. I often put a good tool into people's hands and they're surprised to discover that this is how it's supposed to work."

Chicken city

Home-raised chickens, or at least the idea of them, are all the rage now in some cities. Vancouver recently passed a bylaw allowing backyard chickens, but not without a great deal of angst and bickering and bad chicken puns from those both for and against.

It all seemed out of proportion because not that many people were ever likely to actually take chickens on. They involve more effort than many people expect. Then again, a dog or cat also involves effort, and few pet owners begrudge the fact that they must follow behind their little marvels picking up their poop. In fact, that may be a good way to think of your city chickens — as pets, but ones who happen to regularly provide the makings of omelets. If you've already proven your mettle by keeping a pet dog or cat alive, you should have no trouble handling chickens. Raising hens (your neighbors will thank you for not keeping roosters) is not that difficult and actually fun, and the eggs would be worth it even if it wasn't fun. But keeping any animal involves assuming a level of responsibility you should be aware of and accept before you start.

The recent popularity of city chickens has created a lot of written advice you can find through an internet search or even through magazines devoted exclusively to the task. Coop kits and run plans and feed supplies and vets who handle birds are all increasingly found in cities as more people grow wary of factory eggs and long for a healthy alternative they can raise on their own.

One thing to consider if you want chickens for the eggs is the birds' lifespans. Hens are said to lay an average of two eggs in three days, which is good, but they produce for only two or three years while living for ten or twelve. So at some point you will need to make the call on whether to keep your non-laying darlings around, and if not, precisely how to deal with them. Cities with chicken bylaws have created different strategies to handle this sticky issue. Residents in mine are not allowed to kill their own chickens but are invited to contact a vet who works with birds, or search for an

Get this chicken an agent.

old-bird sanctuary. To determine if you're even allowed to keep chickens you may wish to first check the laws for your area (or not, if you live in one of the cities that still bans the birds — illegal chickens were rife in Vancouver before the law allowing them caught up to the owners).

A few things to consider:

Chickens need a house to sleep in at night. These can be elaborate or rough, cute or ugly, but they must offer the birds protection from predators, which in the city can include dogs, raccoons, foxes, coyotes, raptors and more. If you're building a new facility, and ready to go all out, a concrete floor will prevent rodents and snakes from digging under the fence. The coop should be clean, easily accessible and offer privacy for egg laying. It should keep the hens dry and well-ventilated and be easy for you to maintain. The size of the coop depends on the size of your flock. One to two square feet per hen (or more for larger birds) is recommended. There should be six to ten inches of perch space per bird and at least one nest for every four to five hens.

Chickens also need an outside run — like children, you'd hate to see them cooped up indoors all day. If you're building a run just for the chickens, rather than relying on the backyard fence, some suggest burying the wire at least a foot deep while toeing it outward six inches to stop predators from digging under (toeing the fence means they will dig down into more fencing). This sounds troublesome, but the extra-cautious will point out that owners have had digging critters such as raccoons wipe out their mini-flocks. You might also consider covering the run with mesh wire or netting to prevent raptors from swooping down for a take-out chicken dinner.

Is avian flu a worry? Canadian government veterinarians say small backyard flocks are not a concern as they're unlikely to come in contact with a diseased bird, and in the chance one did get sick, the owner is more likely to notice and take prompt action than if the bird were in a factory together with millions of others.

Besides, chickens are hardy creatures, able to thrive in all kinds of conditions and are not known for getting sick easily.

What about neighbor complaints? We've heard rumors of neighbors so irate they will toss dogs over the fence to attack the hated mother cluckers. I have to confess I find the vitriol odd. I wonder if it doesn't stem from some inherited bias against farming by urbanites who consider themselves sophisticates even though they're really not long off the fields themselves. Chickens are seen as country, smelly, dumb, all the things some city folks associate with rural life, which is of course ridiculous. All the same, if you keep your henhouse clean and presentable, and maybe even offer the neighbors a fresh egg once in a while, they might come around to the point where they'll want chickens of their own.

Grow today, eat whenever you want.

You can too

Once you start growing in volume you may be confronted with the delightful quandary of too much food. Sharing with neighbors is an excellent way to take some of the work off your own hands while keeping up good relations. It could also mean you receive something in return at a later date when you're not so flush. Sharing the harvest is a time-honored custom that probably dates back to our days hunting and gathering for things to bring back to the cave. But even when you've plied those nearby with extra zucchini or tomatoes or cucumbers, you may still have crops by the bagful. This is the time to get into making your own preserves.

Canning food is easy, interesting, results in a harvest you can eat all year round and, oh yes, might kill you. The risk of botulism is not terribly high and it can be easily avoided if you just follow the recipes, but you should pay attention. There are scads of books and internet sites that will give you the details. The general idea boils down to the following.

Material requirements are few. For hot-water canning (as opposed to pressure canning, which calls for a separate machine) you need jars and the right-size sealable lids (both sold in supermarkets around harvest time), a large canning pot to boil the jars in — and not much else, although small additions such as a funnel for hot liquids, a canning rack to hold the jars in the canner and a jar lifter to grab them from the boiling water will all make things easier.

The canning process is fairly basic. To make dill pickles I first choose an appropriate soundtrack, knowing I'll be otherwise occupied for a good chunk of the afternoon: opera and pickles go surprisingly well together. Sterilize the jars and lids in boiling water, then place on the counter. Pack each jar tightly with fresh-picked cucumbers, a clove of garlic, a hot pepper, a grape leaf (rumored to keep pickles crunchy although I have my doubts), pickling spice (buy as such or make your own combination with mustard seeds and black peppercorns and whatever) and fresh dill. Fill with boiled pickling liquid made of water, vinegar and pickling salt in amounts you'll determine from the recipe and the number of jars you have to fill (getting the proper acidity level is important to prevent bacteria, so don't alter the ratio). Put the lids on the jars and boil in the canner for ten minutes or whatever the recipe says. Remove and place on the counter to cool — you may hear a satisfying "pop" indicating a solid seal; sealed lids can also be seen curving downward. If any don't seal, it's not a big deal; just refrigerate and eat within a week or two. The rest can be stored in a cool, dry place and eaten over the next year or more. Some say the pickles will taste good by Thanksgiving but even better by Christmas.

TAKE HOME MESSAGE

Don't mow your dinner away.

CHAPTER 5

THE POPULAR FRONT
PLANT YOUR FOOD FLAG

There comes a time when we wish to liberate all our food-growing opportunities from the tyranny of lawn control. We like turnips, our own turnips, dammit, and we don't care who sees us. Or maybe we do care; we care enough that we want the neighbors to know we're more interested in the Earth and healthy food than a chemical contest over the hue of our lawn. Maybe we even want to push things a little. Since we're getting thick into urban agriculture, which feels like a movement, we want anyone else thinking of plowing ahead to feel encouraged by our example. So we plant the front lawn.

Congratulations. You are now a member of the Popular Front. You are an urban farmer and your house is another link in the chain. Your colleagues in cities around the world welcome you with open arms and extra zucchini.

But what will the neighbors say?

A few may be sore at you. They may think their property values will drop. This is possible, in the eyes of some prospective buyers still bound by twentieth-century ideas about the lawn. It's also possible prices will go up for other prospective buyers who know that good, organic soil is worth paying extra.

This is where the city begins to shift, and perceptions change, and one's place on the planet, even on an urban street, begins to make sense. Every new farmer who plants their front yard creates an outpost in the campaign to feed the city of the future. You are making a statement that we are what we eat and we eat where we live.

Clean up your act

The reminders in this book about aesthetics are even more important when you move to the most public face of your property. As urban agriculture spreads, it may be a good idea to give the campaign a clean-cut image and keep your front-yard farm looking spiffy. You could argue that you don't need to, that the practice of growing food in the city is inherently beautiful already, but that's between you and your neighbors. Even if you don't give a flying fig for their opinions, it might boost the cause if you keep an attractive and tidy operation, creating the kind of front-yard farm that others would want to emulate.

Cleanliness is a good organic strategy anyway, according to Lee McFadyen, an organic farmer I met in British Columbia's Similkameen Valley when I stopped beside an orchard to buy organic peaches. "It's the number one strategy for organic growers to stay ahead of pests and diseases," she explained. A lot of bugs make their home in leaf litter, so removing it can remove them, giving you a chance to break the cycle and stay ahead of the hordes. Inspect your plants regularly to remove and discard any diseased or pest-afflicted parts. Keep tools and anything else that comes in contact with plants or soil clean between tasks so you don't spread pathogens throughout the farm.

Some neighbors, perhaps your unofficial street council on snootiness, may complain that you aren't doing your part in maintaining a respectable lawn. It's hard to remember statistics, but you could try to stop them with a tidbit or two from Ted Steinberg's *Specifically American Green: The Obsessive Quest for the Perfect Lawn* (W. W. Norton, 2006).

Eight alarming facts about lawns

1. North Americans dump ten times more pesticides per acre on lawns than farmers do on croplands.
2. It costs more money per acre to maintain a lawn than to grow corn or rice.
3. Some 40 billion dollars was spent on lawns in North America in 2005 — more than the continent gave in foreign aid.
4. Phosphorus runoff from excess lawn fertilizer contributes to algae blooms in rivers, lakes and the ocean that kill fish.
5. Thirty percent of the water used on the East Coast of the US goes to water lawns.
6. An estimated seven million birds are killed in the US each year by lawn pesticides. Scientists are still trying to figure out if there's a link between pesticides and the mysterious death of millions of honeybees through colony collapse disorder.
7. An estimated 75,000 Americans are injured every year from lawnmowers, about the same as from guns.

Still haven't convinced them? Try this kicker with a Jack Nicholson leer:

8. The average homeowner spends 150 hours a year maintaining his lawn...and only 35 on sex.

Community supported agriculture

Community supported agriculture (commonly referred to by its acronym CSA) is a brilliant way to get growers and buyers together. It saves both sides money because no distributors or other middlemen are involved to remove pieces of the pie. The farmer is guaranteed an income at the start of the season, when he or she needs it most to buy supplies. The consumer pays up front, then

Cam Macdonald.

gets a weekly share of the harvest. The mutual accord tends to be amiable and is often flexible, with buyers providing direct input to the growers that serve to strengthen the relationship.

CSA farmer — Cam Macdonald

Cam Macdonald thought front-yard farming made sense, so he tried it, on someone else's front yard. The artist and part-time caterer recently went through a soul search for a right livelihood to serve a troubled planet. He settled on growing organic food, but how and where when he lived in the city and didn't own land?

Ideas are like windborne seeds; you never know where they'll land. Heidi Gigler and Jug Sidhu heard Cam's story one night at a party, reasoned that they had land right outside their front doorstep in their neighborhood near Main Street, and invited Cam to plant it. So he did, together with three partners in his venture.

The results looked fabulous to anyone who likes real food. Amid the typical lawn-and-perennial yards on the rest of the street one suddenly comes across a mini-farm of row crops. Potatoes, spinach, mustard greens and shallots stand out like a flower in a buttonhole.

The experiment has apparently worked for everyone. Cam and his partners took most of the crop to sell or share but also gave plenty to the homeowners. With the success of that yard they spread to others, setting up a community supported agriculture (CSA) business. The following year Cam's group expanded to serve six customers, each of whom paid $400 for the season, which meant fifteen weeks worth of food. So they grossed $2,400. How much did they net?

"Come on," Cam said with a laugh when I talked to him. "We're farmers, not accountants." Then he explained that they hadn't spent much. A little for seeds and some soil amendments, but that was it, so it was mostly profit. Not much of a profit, admittedly, for four people, but Cam says they could certainly scale up production if they weren't also working other jobs. What it did provide them besides a little money was an education that could turn out to be fruitful: the four decided to buy a real farm, and were just about to make an offer on a ten-acre spread on Vancouver Island.

As for Heidi and Jug, they've been thrilled with the look and taste of their new front yard. "The problem," said Heidi, "is it's hard to keep up with the food." They have given some of the extras away to neighbors, including people they hardly knew before the creation of the front-yard farm. "Now we're having constant conversations," she said. "It's really created a community."

Winter farming

Even a slothful or preoccupied farmer can keep a front yard looking good in summer with just enough weeding to ensure it's the food crops that dominate. The splendor can continue through fall as the plants send out their final fruits or last blazes of color along with seedpods to renew the cycle for the next year. The tricky part is making your yard look good in the off-season, during the late fall, winter and early spring when much of nature has lost its radiant green glow.

Where I live there's no reason to ever stop farming, certainly not just because it happens to be chilly or rainy or even snowy. We may not be planting during the winter, but we can harvest from the things we started in summer for just this reason, enjoying homegrown produce in every month of the year. I'm writing this in November having just eaten fresh green beans with my dinner. Even more impressive will be the collard greens I'll pick in December and the January kale we'll steam and eat with rice and the February turnips we'll cook in a core-warming stew. You may live in a more challenging part of the planet, but if you're near the fringe of a climate zone that's amenable it's worth trying to experiment with glass or plastic covers over your plants. An old window set on bricks to make a cold-frame, a mini-greenhouse made of curved PVC pipes or wire and plastic sheeting, or even a real greenhouse can keep your farm operation active all year.

The Growing Power organization is based in Milwaukee, Wisconsin. When I visited in January it was much colder than what I was used to in Vancouver; snow covered the ground and the city was bare, the kind of real winter I'd almost forgotten about living in the west. Yet Will Allen's hoop houses were packed with green growing things.

"People taste our spinach and say it's the best they've ever had," he announced as we stood in one of the basic structures. Right, I thought, remembering how his career had included a leg as a marketing executive for Proctor & Gamble. On the other hand, it was impressive in that weather just to be standing in one of the productive hoop houses, heated only by a compost pile in each corner. The facility was covered by a double layer of poly, and then there were mini-hoops of wire for plastic sheets to be rolled over the rows as an extra layer of protection during really cold spells.

Maybe that was why the spinach looked oddly short, I figured; they're practically freezing in here. I couldn't resist bending down to try a leaf. Sure enough, it was the sweetest I'd ever tasted. My mind reeled with possible explanations. Maybe the cold was helping the spinach produce more sugars as some kind of defense? Maybe the worm-casting manure he used to power his entire operation provided some kind of micronutrients the spinach I was used to eating didn't get? Or maybe he had some better type of spinach to start with? That last one didn't pan out—it turned out to be the same Savoy variety sold in seed packages in garden centers everywhere.

The key to successful winter harvesting is smart summer planting. You can't simply decide to have a winter garden in October and expect to be eating fresh veggies for Christmas. You have to plant accordingly in July, August and, for some fast-growers, September and perhaps even into October. The rule of thumb for my area is to have the plants grown to mature size by Halloween. Once into November they aren't really going to grow any more, but they will stay the same, as if in cold storage, ready to be picked when you need them.

Cold weather crops to try include broccoli, Brussels sprouts, cabbage, carrots, cauliflower, kale, kohlrabi, leeks, parsnips, spinach and Swiss chard. Some varieties are known particularly for being up for the task, and may even have "winter" or "hardy" in their names.

FIVE REASONS TO PLANT FOR A WINTER HARVEST

1. Fewer pests and diseases.

2. Little or no need to weed or water.

3. Plants protect the soil from erosion.

4. Winter harvesting extends your connection to the living Earth all year long.

5. Frost enhances the flavor of certain crops.

Some of your cold crops will have to be pulled before the ground freezes, while others can survive under a cover such as mulch. If fact, the quickest and easiest way to make your front-yard farm look purposely cared for throughout the winter is to spread a mulch of straw around. The neighbors don't need to know whether there's anything underneath it. Even if you haven't gotten around to a planting scheme by the time the weather turns, your straw-covered rows may still give the impression of something incredible going on.

SOS (save our seeds).

Save our seeds

Letting a few of your best plants go to seed will introduce another aspect to your front-yard farm, one that savvy growers and heritage vegetable aficionados will recognize and appreciate, even if others less aware may see nothing but a mess. Oh well, you can't please everyone. But you can explain that saving seeds puts growers into a timeless bond with our ancestors who had the wisdom to preserve some of the favorite crops we enjoy today. This is important not simply because heritage vegetables are threatened with extinction by the spread of monoculture factory farms, but also because the future of seeds themselves is in peril.

Since the 1990s, just five biotech companies have bought over two hundred seed companies in a race to dominate the market and, by extension, the world's agriculture. Monsanto is the front-runner. Google "Monsanto evil" or "terminator seeds" to get started on why this dark spectre of corporate domination should be resisted. Just twenty years ago, the chemical company that gave the world dioxin and Agent Orange didn't sell a single seed. Now even rivals such as DuPont are accusing it of untoward practices in a march to market control, and at least seven state attorneys were reported to be investigating whether Monsanto's 93-percent share of the genetically engineered soybean market was gained by abusing its powers and locking out competition.

In this case resistance is fertile: after the 2010 Haiti earthquake when Monsanto together with USAID "donated" 460 tons of its hybrid seeds, ten thousand poor farmers took to the streets to protest what they considered an attack on their future. "The foundation for Haiti's food sovereignty is the ability of peasants to save seeds from one growing season to the next. The hybrid crops that Monsanto is introducing do not produce seeds that can be saved for the next season, therefore peasants who use them would be forced to somehow buy more seeds each season," explained Bazelais Jean-Baptiste, an agronomist from the Peasant Movement of Papaye (MPP) who is currently directing the "Seeds for Haiti" project in New York City.

Seed saving can be as easy as watching how your plant matures, then collecting some of the seeds yourself before they drop or waft away in the breeze to new homes. Dry and store in an airtight jar or, for legumes such as beans, in a breathable bag or envelope.

But you need to know what seed you're saving. Hybrid plants, which are increasingly popular as they combine the traits of two parent plants to get desirable features in size, vigor and taste, don't reproduce "true to type." You want to save seeds that are "open pollinated," which may also be labeled OP, non-hybrid, heirloom or heritage. Plants that cross-pollinate, such as spinach, may still not produce true to type if you have another variety of spinach nearby. Self-pollinating plants such as tomatoes, peppers, beans, eggplants and summer squash are most likely to give you what you want if you happen to grow a particularly tasty example. Save the seeds from the healthiest plant you have.

Dirty talk

The very idea of urban agriculture is alarming to some who believe cities are cesspools of pollution. I hear this sentiment more often from seniors than youth, which leads me to wonder if it stems from the once-common notion that rural areas are good and clean and pure and wholesome while cities are bad and dirty and wicked and pestilent. Like any cliché this one may have once held some truth, but if it did, it's less true than it used to be since the factories and mills that once powered cities shut down or moved overseas, and as we learn more about ecology and how to clean up our messes.

But we're not living in an urban paradise yet, so concerns about city food and contaminants are justified. Although not just about city food. As a public health service in 2007, four Canadian federal politicians volunteered to have their blood and urine tested for toxins. To no one's surprise, the politicians turned out to be poison. The researchers found pesticides, stain repellent, flame retardants, arsenic and many more chemicals. *In their blood.* Which means they're probably also *in your blood.* The list included a variety of toxins associated with cancer, developmental problems, hormone disruption and damage to the nervous system. The dramatic among you may now run amok, screaming and clawing at your skin. The rest of us will have to endure one more disturbing fact from the study: the cleanest official among the four had 49 different pollutants coursing through his veins, while the highest had 55.

Sigh. Let's face it. We are a chemical soup. But let's also keep this in perspective. It doesn't mean urban-grown food is inedible. People who worry about eating something grown in their own neighborhood near a road should consider all the food they eat from California grown next to some of the busiest roads in the world, the freeway system.

What to do? Minimize the risks, for sure, but don't abandon

reason ("now everything causes cancer") or give up ("got a ciga-
rette?"). There may even be good news on the personal poisons
beat. Researchers recently tested a large number of Canadians'
blood, and found lead in 100 percent of the subjects. That's not
the good part. Older Canadians had the highest levels of all. That's
not really good either, but it does show that policy can make a
difference. Concentrations of lead in our bodies have fallen dra-
matically over the past thirty years, ever since the government got
serious about regulation and banned lead from paint and gasoline.
Although one in four Canadians had toxic levels of lead three decades ago, today 99 percent of the population is within the limits
considered safe. Meaning that we can, when we get together to
agree on these things, make our cities safer places.

Know the land

If you can find out the history of your food-growing site, you'll
go a long way toward determining how thoroughly you'll need to
check the soil for contaminants.

Cities typically have historical property records that can be
checked through city hall. If your site was once a gas station or a
dry cleaner, a comprehensive test for a wide range of toxins would
be advised. A site that has long been residential may be less of
a problem, although you may still decide to do a test for heavy
metals. Ask around the neighborhood to learn more about the
home's particular history. If it was owned by gardeners, that's
probably good. If it was owned by an amateur mechanic who liked
to fix cars and dump radiator fluid in the yard, not so much.

Check with your extension office, university agriculture department or city hall to find out where soil can be tested locally.
Costs vary depending on the place and on what tests you order.
Basic soil fertility tests, which may include recommendations on
precisely what nutrients to add in what amounts, are the cheapest, about $25 in most places. Adding a test for heavy metals may

run the bill up to $100 or more. Checking for things like PCBs that freak out anyone not wearing a hazmat suit will send the fee higher.

Ultimately, how much you worry is up to you. Plenty of urban growers never test for anything, eat lots of food from their yards and are still standing. Evaluating a risk first involves considering the target. Children, especially those under the age of five, are the most vulnerable to toxins, so if you're thinking of growing in a new place and counting on your young farmhands to help out and eat the produce, adjust your tolerance level accordingly.

Lead out

If you do decide to get your soil tested for heavy metals, don't be surprised when the result comes back showing you indeed have them. The question is how much. As the saying goes, it's not the poison but the dose. Lead, cadmium, mercury, nickel and copper are all commonly found in urban soils. Lead is the most likely offender, especially in older cities. Lead-based paint wasn't banned in the US until 1977, so houses built before then are suspect. Lead is no longer allowed in gasoline, but ongoing sources include industrial emissions, vehicle and tire debris, lead pipes, even lead-based glazes on ceramics.

What if your test comes back showing lead or other metals above acceptable safety levels? Don't panic. You don't have to move. You still have options to reduce the risk of growing food at that site.

Get a lift

The most popular solution is to grow above the problem, using clean soil you bring in. The safest way is to cover the old soil with an impermeable material such as a pond liner and add clean soil on top, or build planting boxes with the bottoms above ground level. Opt for taller fruiting vegetables like tomatoes instead of leafy greens or rooting vegetables. Mulch the area around the growing beds to reduce any lead-contaminated soil you or your pets might track into the home. And be sure to thoroughly wash anything you grow before eating.

This may sound overprotective to some. On the other hand, a study of 141 backyard gardens in Boston found the level of lead in raised beds *rising* over four years from an average 150 micrograms per gram to 336 micrograms — close to the Environmental Protection Agency's safety limit of 400 micrograms. Researchers believe the culprit was fine-grained lead dust wafting up from the contaminated soil surrounding the beds. So the problem was not the food-growing bed itself but the nearby soil. Eating the produce accounted for only 3 percent of the children's daily exposure to lead. The researchers suggested skimming the top three to five centimeters of soil off the raised beds each year and replacing it with compost. Whatever you do, remind your kids to wash their food well before they eat it.

If people learn you're faced with the problem of heavy metals, some will immediately suggest phytoremediation. This is a way to use plants to remove contaminants from the soil. Working with nature is a worthy idea, but the problem here is it takes a lot of plants a long time to get effective results, probably more than a small venture like a front-yard farm can handle. And because heavy metals are elements that don't just disappear, you still have the issue of how to dispose of the plants. Everyone gets nervous when the subject of disposing toxins comes up, perhaps less because of the potential harm to people than the costs that start mounting once lawyers and liability enter the conversation.

Air pollution

People sometimes tell me it's wrong or dangerous to grow food in cities because the air is polluted. To which I respond: Puh-lease! And then: Did you check where your supermarket vegetables came from? Have you been to Mexico City lately? Or Beijing? If I really want to put a thudding stop to the conversation I'll go on to mention something I read in *The Big Necessity: The Unmentionable World of Human Waste* by Rose George (Metropolitan Books, 2008). She mentions the frequent sight of farmers in roadside fields in China spraying the contents of toilets onto cabbages. "The practice would horrify any public health professional, given the disease-load of feces, but it's what happens to 90 percent of China's excrement, and has been done forever. There are reasons not to eat salads in China, and why the sizzling woks are so sizzling."

On the other hand, polycyclic aromatic hydrocarbons (PAHs), a known carcinogen from incomplete combustion, can come from vehicle pollution next to roads or railways, from wood- or coal-burning sites, or from areas that used creosote railroad ties, a popular garden feature in the 1970s and 1980s. Just how PAHs can affect human health is not well known, but frightening all the same. So where does that leave us?

Mean streets

I turned for help to Dr. Art Bomke, a soil specialist at the University of British Columbia's Faculty of Land and Food Systems who has taught thousands of students and knows the joys and challenges of city farming through his generous support for community agriculture ventures. I asked him whether it was safe to grow food beside city roads.

"It all depends. How close to the roadway is the garden? How heavy is the traffic? Is there a residual problem from the era of leaded gas?

"I heard a report in the last couple of days about health concerns regarding manganese. Manganese is an essential element for plants and animals, but too much of it can be toxic. The reason for mentioning it is that it is substituted for lead in gasoline and may be an issue near roads.

"What to do. First, it is likely a good idea to test for lead contamination and possibly hydrocarbons if the garden is near a heavy traffic area. The second issue would be the incoming airborne contaminants from current traffic. This could be on the vegetables. Unfortunately, I don't know of more detailed sources of info, although researchers must be working on this."

Professor Bomke didn't mention it, but I've seen potatoes growing in a half-barrel in front of his house next to the sidewalk. It's not a busy street, but hey, the potatoes are right there.

Home farmer — Iinsoo Park

The Mi Sung Farm is immaculate: bulging green rows of chives, a small sea of sesame leaves in a uniform luminous green, everything looking as neat and trim as a landscaped suburban lawn. Which was apt because Iinsoo Park, the farmer, lives on five acres near Vancouver in a residential area not far from a busy highway intersection.

All the young people looking for a way into farming and then a way to turn it into a career, and here I stumbled along a busy street by accident onto someone doing just that. His home looked good, a modern two-story affair with an SUV and a minivan in the driveway.

Iinsoo Park.

Park explained that he had been a physical education teacher back in Korea. That sounded like good training for his current career, but he just sighed, saying farming was "a lot of work."

He grows on about half of his property. There were some greenhouses in the back, but we talked in the front yard as he cut chives into bundles. Like everything he grows, they were for the local market, and would be delivered early the next morning.

"Too much work," he said again when I complimented him on how orderly everything seemed. He wore a uniform of sorts, not the farmer overalls of North America but a lightweight water-shedding shirt and pants with the cuffs tucked into his socks. On his knees were kneepads, a sensible idea professional landscapers adopt when they have a lot of in-ground handwork to do. They know that kneeling beats bending over all day.

Park didn't have the same enthusiasm for urban agriculture some newcomers express. "Seven days," he replied when I asked him to describe his workweek. "Today? I woke up today at 6 AM. Now it's 6 PM and I'm still working. I have to cut these chives when it's cool. If I cut them during the daytime they may dry out before I get them to the market. Some mornings I wake up at 4:30. I work until, well, it depends. If I have to deliver food the next day, sometimes I work until midnight."

It was indeed sounding like a lot of work. Surely he had help?

"No, I don't get much help. Several people. Myself and my wife."

Why did he get into it in the first place?

"I came here and I had the land, so I started farming."

Would he recommend it to others?

"Hmm. Depends on the person. I was a teacher in Korea. Teaching physical education. I think teaching is better. This is too much work. It's all physical work."

I will say this much: he seemed in great shape.

Political farmer — Harold Steves

Harold Steves, who you may remember from Chapter 3 promoting organics, is a front- and back- and side-yard farmer leading urban agriculture into a new era. He's either one of the last rural farmers or first urban farmers in the Vancouver area: the changeover happened on his watch. The farm begun by his great-grandfather on rich delta soils in Richmond was once rural but gradually became surrounded by suburbia.

"The Steveston Stock and Seed Farm has been our official name for a hundred years. I'm not sure when we became an urban farm but when we did we figured, okay, we've got to fight for urban agriculture."

We talked at his kitchen table, always a good place to hear farmer tales, and during a stroll around his grounds. We paused to admire his Belted Galloway beef cattle sticking out in the suburban neighborhood like costumed guests at a party that isn't masquerade after all. We also checked out his fruit trees, a few of which he replanted with grafts from the originals that had collapsed but weren't quite dead. He wasn't sure how old the originals were, but noted they were part of the yard for a farmhouse built in 1877.

Harold Steves.

Our stroll continued with talks about apple wine — an alternative to cider, in which you boil diced apple with sugar and water, strain the result to get a liquid and then ferment into wine — as well as detours to check on his seed-producing plants, including sprouted leeks, a variety of rutabaga from Scandinavia and yellow mangel, which I'd never heard of before. Later I did some research and found that yellow mangels are not common, though I did find a reference in an 1879 edition of *American Agriculturalist* that also had ads for steam engines and butter churns.

Steves explained: "The yellow mangel is like a sugar beet. Sugar beets were grown in World War II to produce sugar since we couldn't get sugar from cane down south. The mangel is a big yellow beet. They're just like a garden beet only they're ten pounds and taste sweeter. And the leaves are fantastic. You can cook them just like spinach."

Why aren't we all eating mangels?

"Nobody's ever heard of them. So we specialize in mangels. We grow about five different varieties of mangels. Four varieties are for cattle. They were used for hundreds of years in Europe in

The cows can still come home in the city of Richmond, British Columbia, at the Steveston Stock and Feed Farm.

winter as feed for livestock. England and Scotland are famous for growing turnips for cattle. Hay storage and silage are not all that dependable, but you could store these in the ground. It takes a lot of work growing them, so people got lazy and it became a hay and silage culture. But originally it used to be every dairy farmer would have a field of these mangel beets. We've maintained the cattle variety but you can't eat the leaves of those, they're not as sweet. But the yellow mangel is almost like a gourmet beet. They're quite tasty. Everyone we've given them too loves them and wants some more seed."

You can't talk for long about seeds with a farmer, especially one as committed as Steves, before you get into the bigger picture. Steves said the backstory behind the yellow mangel touches on the global seed industry.

"We didn't know we were going to be doing war against Monsanto in the end but that's what it turned out to be. All we knew was the main company that carried the same seeds my grandfather did fifty years earlier went out of business and the seed stock just disappeared. These were varieties that had been experimented on by my family and other growers who grew them out successfully in the Fraser Valley going back a hundred years. These are the varieties of vegetables adapted to these soils in this climate. So we thought, there's something wrong with this. If all the seed stocks in the world controlled by big international agricultural companies are for planting in Mexico where the climate is quite different, what would happen if we wanted to grow these crops here? We wouldn't be able to take their seed and grow it here; the poor little plants would die of fright for the cold, or whatever. We started thinking we'd better start saving these northern varieties because we may need to grow them again some day. This started in '82. We got in touch with the Seed Savers Exchange, and we've since built up to about 75 varieties of heirloom, variety vegetables."

Steves doesn't just spout ideas; he acts on them. When he came home from university one day in the late 1950s to find his father explaining that their rural farm area had just been declared residential, which meant they weren't allowed to upgrade to a bigger

Walk This Way

Brooklyn Grange is a rooftop operation that's actually in Queens. It's a for-profit enterprise growing food to sell in the city, but also keen on showing school groups, families, volunteers and anyone else interested how to grow food in a big city. "This is a green space that contributes to the overall health and quality of life of the community, bringing people together through green business and around good food."

Examples & Inspiration

— **brooklyngrangefarm.com** —

dairy, he got farmers together to seek a solution. This eventually led to the province's admirable Agricultural Land Reserve, and later led Steves to run for the Richmond City Council, a position he still serves in today.

He considers himself a farmer first and politician second, and looks the part with his jeans and boots, but I wondered whether he had any regrets about all that time spent slogging in council chambers.

"No. It's just that the end results are very slow. The things we were trying to do in '68 we're still trying to do today. Forty years is a long time to achieve your objectives. But suddenly I think we've got a good chance. Many of the predictions we made are coming true. We get visitors from around the world who show up to see how we've saved our farmland. So it is envied all around the world.

"At the time I was concerned we were only producing 86 percent of our vegetables. Now we grow something like 43 percent of our own food."

So people can and will grow food again?

"Yes. And that gets back to us with seed saving. We're saving seeds that will grow here. You can't say that with Monsanto. You won't be able to be food self-sufficient if they're genetically selecting plants to grow in Mexico or California or wherever. That's why the two go hand in hand. We need to maintain our land and our seed stock and our ability to grow our own food."

Can you grow all your own food?

"We've grown pretty much all our vegetables for last twenty or thirty years. You sure save some money if you grow all your own food. Not just as an experiment, it's a tremendous monetary advantage when you add up the food budget and see how much you've saved."

Farmers' markets are great but they can be expensive.

"Exactly. The farmers' market is great for buying local, which I think more people should do, but the ultimate is to grow your own food. If you can grow your own food with varieties acclimatized to this climate and put recyclable materials back into the soil again you'll have very nutritious food because you aren't using chemical fertilizers. It just has so many advantages. It saves money, helps the environment and the list goes on and on."

Bee farmer — Assefe Kebede

Some people don't feel they're properly on a farm unless it has animals. I'm not one of them, but am usually happy to see living beasts that can be eaten (even if I don't eat them), especially if their waste is recycled back into the nutrient system to bring the farm as close as possible to a closed loop.

Assefe Kebede.

We've mentioned fish and chickens and worms so far. Another possibility to get living things working for you is bees.

The practice of beekeeping involves more detail than we can go into here. Most newcomers start out by taking a course. The techniques are not all that difficult, but everyone seems to agree the courses are valuable. A few nights of lectures, a few visits to actual hives, a little homework, maybe a test to make sure you're weren't sleeping through the whole thing, and then you just need to get your bees and supplies and you're on your way to the land of honey.

Assefe Kebede showed me his front-yard bees as a way to explain how simple it can be. Originally from Ethiopia, he now operates an African food restaurant in Vancouver and works as a project manager, so he doesn't sound like the kind of guy who has a lot of spare time. But his hives were doing well.

"It's mostly getting everything set up," he said as we sampled some of his bees' work over home-baked bread. "When you put everything in place, the bees take care of the rest. Unless you have a problem."

Busy bees do much of the work for you.

Mites are one problem found lately in many hives in British Columbia, a concern because they're lethal to the bees. These may or may not be related to colony collapse disorder, that eerie die-off of many bees all over the world. I thought it was largely a North American issue until a recent trip to Asia, in which I heard the same thing is happening there. Like the mystery of frogs dying in droves planet-wide, this is definitely something to keep an eye on.

Another thing that could happen is your bees may swarm. The visual effects of this can be arresting—imagine a great cloud of buzzing, swirling bees attached to your neighbor's porch swing. The swarm is actually less scary than it sounds—the bees have merely separated from the hive with a new queen and are too busy house-hunting to be interesting in stinging things—but it still takes a beekeeper with some nerve to go collect them.

"Anyway, it's worth it," Kebede allowed, dripping another luscious spoonful onto a chunk of bread, and I had to agree with him. Anyone who likes the unmatched taste of fresh city-flower honey, or is fascinated by the politics of the hive, should keep bees. Check your area for the next workshop and buzz in. The more people we get keeping bees, the more allies our industrious little friends can enlist to overcome the hard times ahead.

TAKE HOME MESSAGE

Put food up front.

CHAPTER 6

Homeowners with lawns that can be dug under make up a small portion of the world's city growers. The yardless are on the rise. Every week the global urban population swells by a million people, not many of whom are troubled over which lawnmower to buy. So this chapter is for everyone, land-secure or not. This is where we look beyond our own living spaces in our quest to get more food from the city. You may want to do this for production reasons, since more land can produce more crops. You may want to do this for political reasons, because you see food as a critical design element for the future of an urban planet. Anyone out to save the world must consider how it works beyond his or her own space. In this chapter we examine how to get more food from the places we share, from the untended lot, the school yard, and beyond, or above.

Wild food farmer — Yona Sipos

You can have your city and eat it too with wild food foraging. Four years ago when I was researching *Guerrilla Gardening: A Manualfesto* I decided to explore what was actually in an "empty"

Yona Sipos.

lot. I invited a plant biologist to tour it with me, and as he spoke I scribbled down dozens of Latin botanical names that he said traced the history of Western civilization as written in the species spread by European settlers and their agriculture.

For this book I invited another plant biologist to the same lot, this time one who leads nature walks into forests to teach people about the bounty around us, including the edibles. Yona Sipos is a doctoral candidate at the Faculty of Land and Food Systems at the University of British Columbia. We spoke on the street beside the lot. She told me how she got into eating the great outdoors, urban-style.

"I made it my business to know wild foods because I think it's important. There's a lot of food to be found in city lots. Some you might only eat in dire circumstances, but there's also a lot you can eat to enjoy, maybe with enough salt and spices. I did my undergraduate degree in plant biology and

That "empty" lot may be a feast in waiting.

ecology. I didn't get a whole lot of field experience, but I worked in labs, and worked with other students who were interested, and in summertimes we would gather salads on the way home. So we just learned on the road, so to speak. And tried to stay away from the road, actually."

About those roads: is food collected in the city safe to eat?

"We have to weigh our risks in the cities. On a busy corner of a busy city there are inherent risks. I would not eat a plant right beside the road. There's a good chance it could have gasoline spilled on it or oil or bottom-of-the-car dirt, not to mention animals or people peeing on it. Not that pee is necessarily a bad thing, but I would definitely rinse things off."

Now that we've grossed everyone out...how far away from the road?

"When we have a chance to plant it, and we think about plants as biological filters, we look at the first couple of layers as being able to trap or filter a lot of the smog, or at least able to uptake part of it. Like farmers along busy roads who plant a row of trees to block pollution and smog, it's the same idea when foraging for food."

The first layer for this lot was a blackberry vine, the tough but sweet juvenile delinquent of the northwest plant world, hanging out in a crowd as usual no matter how rough the neighborhood. We stepped through a gap into the lot, to be faced with an old futon, a broken video camera, strewn papers and the remnants of a small fire.

Plants covered most of the detritus with green. Sipos described them as "typical of city lot in an urban environment on the west coast. Himalayan blackberry isn't native, but is now what we typically find in disturbed spots. It is an invasive but on the other hand it's so tasty it's hard to dismiss."

Unfortunately there were no berries to munch on—the season was long past. We saw mostly young cottonwood trees about twice our height.

"Also not surprising," Sipos said. "Cottonwood indicates that this is probably a bit of a wet site — information that may be more interesting to builders and city zoners than wild food foragers. As far as I know you can't eat cottonwood for nutritional value, so it won't fill you up. But if you have a headache you could try brewing a cottonwood tea — the salicylic acid is related to aspirin."

That made me wonder just what we mean when we say one plant is edible but another isn't.

"We can define edible in a few ways. Probably the most simple is that it won't kill you or harm you. So we can ingest it, ideally with some good nutritional or medicinal properties. It can also be edible in one form but something has to be done with the original product, like stinging nettles, a plant you could say was edible but you have to steam it first."

I was still puzzled about why we could eat nettles but not other plants that look very similar. Maybe there are other factors, like taste?

"Actually taste is a pretty good indicator. Our bodies are pretty good at making a broad distinction between what is good to eat and what is harmful. Often what is poisonous will be really bitter or dry your mouth out. If you're ever not sure about a plant, take a tiny bit between your teeth and chew on it a bit and then spit it out. Just sit with it for ten to twenty minutes. If you have any weird or uncomfortable sensations, obviously you wouldn't eat more. But if that's okay you can taste a tiny bit more, giving yourself time to check it out.

"As for what our bodies can digest and use for nutrition, that's phytochemistry, which is not my area, but it gets to how much glucose is in there, how much carbon is in there. Also whether it has a lot of cellulose, which is a structure in plant cell walls we can't digest. Cows can eat grass because they have an extra stomach but we can't."

We came across a patch of clover, something you see everywhere. I didn't realize it could be eaten.

"It's edible but not necessarily the tastiest. This one is common red clover. Like white clover, it's found often in fields. The leaves and flowers, when they're young and more tender, can be eaten fresh, especially if you have a little lemon and salt to break up the cell walls a bit. Or you can steam them. They're fine for salads. Because they're in the legume family they're actually a good source of protein.

"I see some dandelions. You often find asters of various kinds in city lots. Dandelions are edible earlier in season. A lot of aster leaves, when young and tender, make good salad greens, again with some salt and lemon to break up the cell walls. Oh! There's some lamb's quarter. That's in the Chenopodiaceae family, which also includes quinoa. A lot of the plants in that family have edible seeds, although you may not want to consume them in large quantities because they're not always good for digestion. Lamb's quarter grows often in city lots. They're especially good in spring when tender."

I had thought we might exhaust the list with three or four species, given that it was already fall, but Sipos kept rattling them off.

"There's some equisetum [horsetail], which you can use to make tea, but you're not supposed to drink it over an extended period of time. It has silica in it, which is why horsetail is a good plant to use when washing pots. For a cleanse, you can boil it in water and let it steep for half an hour. It actually tastes pretty good.

"Here's some plantain. It was called white man's footsteps because it came with the colonizers. Like many of the plants here, it originated in Europe. It's actually a good headache remedy too. White men used to take a plant and tie it with a red ribbon around their forehead.

"There is some St. John's wort. When you hold up the leaves or flowers you can see little dots where light comes through—that's how you identify it. That and the yellow flower with five petals. You can make a tea by steeping the leaves. It's supposed to give a sense of well-being.

"There's also some bamboo. I don't know much about it, but people eat the fresh bamboo that comes up in spring, so maybe this one is edible too."

With all that, along with a curious vine of hops taking up a corner of the fence that made us wonder if a home brewer lived nearby, I thought we did pretty well. This was the mild form of wild foraging, something one can do almost as a pastime. There's a more active form practised by people who call themselves freegans, or free vegans, in a form of anti-consumerist vegetarian-ism that maintains tossing good food into dumpsters is wrong. So they liberate it, and eat free meals at the same time.

Judge the dumpster divers if you will. But if you're going to criticize anyone, include all of us who support a society and a food system in which an estimated half of the food grown to harvest size never gets eaten.

Cover crops

Patches of bare earth don't do anything for the farmer, or for the living earth, as the rain washes nutrients away. You can help both and turn drab scenes into lively landscapes by planting cover crops in late summer or early fall (or in spring for sections you won't otherwise be using for crops that season). They not only look good, and can attract beneficial insects, they also loosen and aerate the soil while adding nutrients to it, which is why they're also sometimes called green manure.

Some urban growers have taken to helping barren or weed-infested lots start on the transition to greater fertility by broadcast-seeding with cover crops. The seeds aren't expensive so you won't be out much even if the space gets taken over later by something unrelated to food. In the meantime you and everyone else can en-joy the site of undulating green waves (and perhaps later, flowers) wafting in the breeze, while a few in the know will understand the real significance of the changes happening within the soil.

It makes good environmental sense to let nature do the work

of fertilizing your soil for you, rather than bringing it in at the expense of fossil fuels and greenhouse gas emissions. In my region with its reliable fall rains, we can just scatter the seeds, rake them in and walk away. The following spring, two to three weeks before planting time, we turn the cover crops into the soil and all systems are go.

Cover crop choices are many, and can even be applied in blends such as oats mixed with winter peas.

Buckwheat, which will sprout and grow quickly in spring and summer to cover a space that might otherwise have been taken over by weeds, will also attract bees and other beneficial beasts if left to flower.

Crimson clover will help fix nitrogen into the soil, reducing or eliminating the need to buy fertilizer. If you leave it in the ground until the following June it will flower in a way that looks great and makes your local pollinators including honeybees happy. Turn it under before the flower color starts to fade if you want to prevent it from re-seeding.

Fall rye germinates in cool soil so it can be planted later than most cover crops. The vigorous roots loosen soil to improve drainage. Rye is not difficult to turn under if you do it early enough. After about mid-March it can get fairly tough and perhaps require

SIX REASONS TO PLANT COVER CROPS

1. Improve soil health.
2. Prevent erosion.
3. Suppress weeds.
4. Increase organic matter.
5. Improve microbiotic activity, soil structure and water infiltration rate.
6. Provide habitat for beneficial insects.

chopping down before digging in. Wait three weeks after you dig it in before planting your vegetable seeds — rye puts out a chemical to suppress the growth of competing plants.

Downtown farmer — Doris Chow

United We Can is best known for helping low- or no-income people in downtown Vancouver get into recycling. Binners who scavenge the streets and garbage bins for recyclable containers turn them in for cash. In 2010 the organization branched out by transforming a downtown parking lot into an urban farm with the aim of growing food while also training people in job skills. It's called Save Our Living Environment Food, or SOLEfood.

The site is a formerly degraded parking lot next to a dodgy hotel. The SOLEfood group, a blend of social enterprisers and aspiring farmers, was given a short-term lease for the lot from the owner, who some consider a slumlord, in return for their paying his property taxes. Soon as the boxes were built, even without raising a single radish, the project could have been considered an environmental asset, since the growing beds were now absorbing

Doris Chow.

all the rain that would have fallen onto the asphalt and then gone into the storm sewer system on its way to the ocean. And the parking lot certainly looks more appealing. Instead of junked-out cars and trash it's now row upon row of raised bed boxes, many with hoop covers to extend the season.

Doris Chow, one of the farm coordinators, was pleased to explain the operation the afternoon I dropped by. It was a public selling day, when they open from two to six in the afternoon for drop-in sales. A hired helper was preparing lettuce, arugula, Swiss chard and tomatoes. Doris explained that the farm doesn't use volunteers. She said she was one of two paid coordinators, and there were five part-timers hired from the neighborhood. The farm was also getting logistic help from Michael Abelman, a former Californian organic grower who now farms on an island not far from Vancouver when he's not writing books or lecturing.

The group has constructed about 150 planter boxes on the half-acre parking lot farm. Will Allen's approach to pavement parking lots may have been more economically sound, especially given the fact SOLEfood is on borrowed land. Allen uses a layer of wood chips on top of the asphalt, topped by a layer of worm compost, in these dimensions:

- 8 inches of wood chips
- 24 inches of rich compost
- 36-inch-wide mounded bed
- 18-inch path

And that's it: you're ready to plant. But the boxes SOLEfood uses have two advantages: they look nice (which may be important in

Doris Chow in downtown Vancouver.

certain city areas) and they provide a base to hold PVC hoops on which to place row covers that warm up the soil and crops underneath.

"All the food is sold at farmers' markets, three per week," Doris explained. "We have three restaurants on board purchasing food and one afternoon of on-site sales. The on-site sales are more to get people out to actually see the production of a farm. In the city not many people see farms. This kind of alters the perception of what a farm is and how it can function, and educates people about food and food security, which is not only the global food system but also how it functions right here in the Downtown Eastside."

Sales from the produce pay the part-timers' wages. "The capital cost, the initial building cost for the lumber, the soil, the hoops, all of that was one-time grants, corporate grants that were given to us, donations and stuff. The whole goal is to have it be self-sustaining after the one-time grants so that we don't have to rely on constant grants."

They are also confronting perceptions among some that farms and cities do not go together. At least that's what some of the business community has commented for public input on the group's application to spread the farm to an unused section of city land nearby.

"Then there is our whole social aspect. Hiring people from the Downtown Eastside has been quite difficult. There's a perception of what the neighborhood is like. The inner city is the place that needs it most, but to some people there's one image of the Downtown Eastside and the people who are here even though they're actually much more diverse than that and the neighborhood is much more complex than that. For a lot of our employees this place offers an anchor and stability. There's a therapeutic and a rehabilitative aspect in growing. They can see the fruits of their labor that they wouldn't be able to find anywhere else for the fact that nobody would even give them the opportunity."

Go garlic

Garlic is a simple way to get people interested in growing and learning more about their own food. Some think of garlic as a single familiar taste, but growers know that, like wine, it comes in countless flavors to be nurtured and savored.

If you get a variety of garlic that has all the properties you like in flavor, heat, size and so on, it's worth setting aside some cloves to plant (hopefully you bought organic garlic, or at least a type that hasn't been commercially sprayed to prevent sprouting).

There's very little to growing garlic, which is much the point for some. It tends to be hardy and able to ward off pests, making it a good companion plant to keep things away from your less-robust crops. It can be a good choice for an otherwise unused space because it doesn't need constant fussing over. One healthy afternoon of digging in fall could turn a long boulevard strip or abandoned lot green and growing for the next eight or nine months.

Garlic should be planted in well-draining soil in a sunny place. Separate the bulb into cloves and plant each clove, pointy-end up, about two inches deep, leaving enough room between the cloves for mature plants to develop (each plant will produce a bulb). In my area we can plant them any time from September throughout the winter and into spring. They get whatever start the rest of the season offers, hunker down during the cold months, then take off in spring. It doesn't seem to matter when you plant as they all mature around the same time anyway, in mid-July. When the tops start to brown, yank the whole thing out and hang it up to cure for two weeks in a protected place.

School farms

What better way to start raising new generations of farmers than by replacing the acres of pavement or gravel covering our school yards with teaching gardens or farms?

The potential benefits of school farms are so encouraging that people are apt to get all misty at the very idea. Our innocent dears growing their own healthy alternative to McDonald's, our high schoolers paying more attention to carrots than their cell phones, the chance to link the school with the surrounding community through water-sharing duties in the summers, and so on.

Problem is, misty-eyed sentiment doesn't plant seeds, people do, and in the schools these days the people, meaning teachers, are run ragged. Even so, the idea is so appealing to some you may be able to find teacher-champions willing to somehow find the time to take the project on. They will need to be supported by school administrators, facilities staff, students, neighbors, funders and more. Only after everyone has met and agreed to a plan and to share the work should a school garden be attempted. Once it is, though, don't be surprised at how well things can grow. Students who get hooked can bring an incredible amount of pent-up energy into the outdoor project.

Teacher farmer — Brent Mansfield

Brent Mansfield is a school garden coordinator, one of the few positions like it he knows of in North America, and certainly the only one at a school that needs an upside-down question mark to complete its name ("because that's the closest-looking thing"). He's at Grandview/¿Uuqinak'uuh Elementary School in inner-city Vancouver, bringing hands-on environmental lessons to kids from kindergarten through grade seven.

Like a lot of things with urban agriculture, where one idea can spread to other, sometimes surprising, fields, the idea is taking off in its second year. Some of this is due to Mansfield's enthusiasm, which is infectious.

"Last year the teachers were kind of, 'hmm, whatever,' and this year we just had a staff meeting and they were all excited: 'Let's put in a pumpkin patch! What about a corn maze!' The teachers have really gotten into the concept."

Grandview/¿Uuqinak'uuh has 15 raised garden beds, an ethno-botanical garden, a community garden, a variety of fruiting shrubs and a new composting machine (like the one at Windemere High School). They're wondering about hiring a farmer to grow food for the school on the grounds, and about fronting a year-round weekly salad bar, maybe with the use of a hoop house to keep the greens growing all winter.

Did he say salad bar? That would have that green stuff?

"I have yet to find something kids won't eat. If they're involved with planting it or even seeing it grow, they will eat it. I have had to say, 'Stop eating broccoli, we have to save some so everybody gets to try.' When I brought a broccoli plant inside and it still had all the little flowering stems sprouting up, they were like locusts all over it.

"One day the lunch lady saw the kids swarming one of our greens, she said, 'What dip are you using?' I said, 'Who needs dip?' Kids like things simple and fruits and veggies taste better without dip."

The students will also accept vegetables as learning tools, although it may be best not to introduce them using that term.

"Now we're incorporating food into lessons. Nutrition, for example. What do we get from yellow and orange vegetables?

Brent Mansfield.

Vitamins A and C. What do we get from green vegetables? Vitamins B and E. Green is everything, so green leafy vegetables have a lot of good things for you. Are we done with the lesson? No. Now we go outside and try eight different varieties of green leafy vegetables that kids get to pick themselves and try to find out which ones are their favorites. So those green leafy vegetables? Guess what, they're the same ones we're serving in lunch at the salad bar.

"Sure the kids will eat at the salad bar. I find the simpler the better. Raw kale, mustard greens, chard, spinach, five varieties of lettuce.

"You have to time it properly. We're still experimenting. I want things that will be ready to eat in May–June and in September–October, things that we can pick as late as possible. Like zucchini that's ready now."

We were talking in mid-September, at the start of the school year. He had just asked a class of sprout-sized kiddies to identify a vegetable in the garden. Most of them got it: cucumber. Then he pointed to the leaves of another, and got blank stares because it hadn't fruited yet. "What do the leaves look like?" he prompted. "Cucumber," came the answer. "Right, they look like it, but they're cousins. Does anyone here have a cousin? Well this one is related but it's a little different. Any guesses? Anyone? It starts with a z." A girl shouted out as if she'd nailed it: "Zucumber!" Which wasn't right but might be a better name than zucchini.

"My lesson is: unless school gardens become central to learning and the life of the school, they will die. There is no curriculum subject you cannot teach through the garden. And teach in a powerful and engaging way. We can also teach things we realize as a society need to be taught, but we don't teach well. Things like food security and sustainability. By teaching through the garden you do it in a way that includes a powerful connection to the Earth. You can teach about health, nutrition. It's a participatory nutritional education.

"Every teacher here is involved in the garden. It's great for anything, even math. Kids will learn math for two hours and not even realize they've been learning math. Take kale that's gone to seed. Now it's like a big tree, one with many seedpods. Suppose you had to estimate how many seeds it had. Estimation, that's a super difficult concept to get across, but with the seedpods you can do it. Start by cracking open one of the seedpods. This is actually a really handy thing to have if you have a kid with behavioral problems because they get absorbed by the tiny seeds. So let's say you count and there are 20 to 45 seeds. Now we have a data set. We can count a few more seedpods to see how the numbers work out. Now we have mode, medium, mean. If we're looking for a total, we'll want to work out an average number of seeds per pod, maybe it's 35, and multiply it by the estimated number of seedpods. We might end up with a number like 25,000 — now we're also teaching the miracle of growing, that one seed can produce 25,000 more just like it. It's all done using math."

Up on the roof

Looking down from a skyscraper or an airplane over any big North American city, you're apt to be struck by all the wasted space on rooftops. Acres of food could be grown right in the busiest districts of our cities if we can just put get the simple equation of empty space (roofs) and needed space (farms) together.

Of course it isn't that easy, as many of the buildings will not have been engineered to endure a heavy load of soil, water, crops and farmers. But anything with a flat roof has been designed to take a heavy snowfall (or perhaps a rain storm, depending on where you live), so it isn't as if you could collapse the thing with a few containers filled with food.

We are still in the early years in the development of green roofs in North America. Europe is ahead, particularly the practical Germans. Japan is catching up, but in sometimes wild ways. I toured a new four-story building in a busy district that had a rice paddy

Sky-high food grown on roofs in Vancouver (above) and Tokyo (below).

on the top. The owner, originally from the countryside, wanted rice, and he got it, along with a neat vegetable garden on the side.

New buildings can and should be designed to accept the weight of plants and their growing medium. Some governments have legislated a certain percentage of building tops that must include green roofs. Unfortunately they don't always specify which type of green roof is desired. The trend is to use the lightest growing medium in the shallowest space, resulting in the hardy but ubiquitous sedum. The roof does indeed become green, and it somewhat serves its purpose in aesthetics and in absorbing storm water and cooling the surroundings. But every time I see another of these sterile sedum sites I lament the opportunity lost. Why not turn it into a farm? A place for a people and plants to work together? A place the building's occupants and others will go to often for food or leisure or both?

The proof is in the peppers.

There are some fine examples of rooftop food gardens in cities around the world. We just need more of them. As it stands now, people are not accustomed to using their roofs. And so they don't. I've seen fantastic gardens with lots of sun and incredible views and boxes all set up and planted...only to be left to go to seed because the original growers moved on and the people who came next didn't care. Something about going up to the roof seems to pass them by—I think it's less an active refusal than the fact that the roof is out of sight and out of mind. We will eventually become more frequent roof farmers, but we're not there yet.

You can get started on the campaign by turning whatever available roof space you find into food-producing sites. Even a pot with a tomato is something. The challenges of rooftop growing may become apparent. A farm in the sky is a different place than the one directly below it in the ground. It's usually hotter, windier and drier. So you want to be sure you have your irrigation figured out, either through a timed system or through diligence to keep things in check.

These challenges can of course be turned into advantages. A community garden project I've been involved with for the past year found its home on the roof of a downtown hospital. Grown in a mix of organic soil and compost that was wheeled *through* the hospital to the roof by gardeners nonchalantly pushing covered recycling barrels, the full sun and lack of pests produced bumper crops that astonished the newer growers, and may have helped turn some into lifelong urban farmers.

Walk This Way

Examples & Inspiration

The world's best-known organic farmer does it as a side job. Michelle Obama gave city farming everywhere a lift when she tore up 1,100 square feet of the White House lawn to grow vegetables. White House compost, White House beehives, White House homegrown organic food served at official state dinners: ever get the sense the First Couple is cooler than you? This transcript from the White House press office describes the First Lady's conversation with schoolchildren who helped to plant the seeds. She has already asked why it's important, and heard the kids say that eating fruits and vegetables gives you more energy and make you strong.

Mrs. Obama: *It can make you strong — yes, absolutely. This is one of the main reasons we're doing this. What I've learned as a mom, in trying to feed my girls, is that it is so important for them to get regular fruits and vegetables in their diets, because it does have nutrients, it does make you strong, it is all brain food. And when you go to school, it is so important for you to have a good breakfast, to make sure in your lunches that you have an apple or*

an orange or a banana, that you have something green when you
eat any meal, lunch or dinner.

And we're looking to you guys to help educate the country, not just
in your own homes, but other people as they think about how to
plan their meals for their kids, to think about the importance of
making sure that we have enough fruits and vegetables. And doing this garden is a really inexpensive way of making that happen.
Do you know how much—I mean, look how big this garden is.
Do you know how much it costs to just do this? And we're going
to have carrots and spinach and herbs and berries. We're going to
have a ton of stuff in this garden. How much do you think it costs
to do this garden? How much?

Child: Over $100,000.

Mrs. Obama: Over $100,000. (Laughter.) My husband would go
crazy—(laughter)—if he thought we were spending that kind of
money. No, a little lower than that. How much do you think? You.

Child: I think $5,000?

Mrs. Obama: $5,000? No, a little lower. Yes.

Child: $1,000?

Mrs. Obama: $1,000? No.

Child: $200.

Mrs. Obama: $200—it doesn't—it hasn't cost us more than $200
to plant this.

Child: $100?

Mrs. Obama: It's about $100—it's between $100 and $200. So it's
not a lot of money. And this garden can not only feed my family,
but it's going to feed all the staff at the White House. We're going
to use these vegetables to help feed you guys. We're going to serve
it at some state dinners. So with this little plot of land—and this
is a big plot; you don't even have to plant this much—we can
produce enough fruits and vegetables to feed us for years and
years to come—for just a couple of hundred dollars. Now, isn't that
amazing?

> *So we're looking to you guys to help us make it happen. So we're going to plant the seedlings today. And then in a few months, hopefully right around the time you get out of school, you can come and help us harvest the fruits and vegetables, and come into the White House with all of our chefs and start doing a little cooking. How does that sound?*
> **Children:** *Good.*

First planting plan for the First Yard.

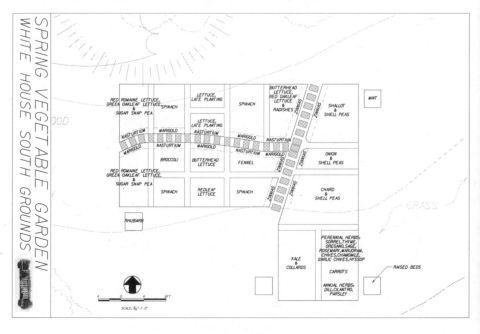

TAKE HOME MESSAGE

Every radish is a statement.

CHAPTER 7

RETURN OF THE COMMMONS
GROWING COMMUNITY

The idea of public space as something we have a right or even a duty to care about has withered. How and why this happened is difficult to understand, because it didn't come down by decree or all at once, but by a thousand corporate cuts. Every time a private interest chips away at our shared places, and we do nothing, we end up that much weaker as a society.

The tragedy of the commons is a conceptual model suggested by Garret Hardin in the journal *Science* in 1968. It describes a cow pasture shared by a community of cow owners. Individual owners send their cows to the pasture to graze, which works fine so long as there are a few owners with a few cows, but as the numbers grow, the pasture gets crowded, and eventually destroyed. The tragedy is supposed to be that the commons doesn't work for a crowded pasture, or planet, because people will look out for their individual needs before those of the community. The essay is still used to get people to ponder the Earth's growing population and the Malthusian fears of hunger from many mouths to feed. But it turns out that's not the case. Hunger is not a problem of quantity: we grow enough food to feed everyone already. We actually have

There's more than vegetables growing in a community garden.

a surplus. It's a problem of poverty: the poorest can't afford it. So it's the system that's flawed. The tragedy in the essay is caused not by the commons but by rampant individualism. Hardin himself once said he should have titled his essay "The Tragedy of the Unregulated Commons." The key is getting the community to agree on how to manage public space. This starts with the notion that there *is* a public space, that we even *have* a commons, and that it is good. It may also include the notion that the land we share needs healing, and farmers are the ones we need to heal it.

Growing community

Many hands make light work, the saying goes, and that holds true for the campaign to transform our cities into city-farms. An interesting aspect of the present rise in urban agriculture will be to see how unique city styles influence the way we collectively grow, harvest, package, sell, eat and recycle food. Cities are social centers of innovation, cultural gumbos filled with a diversity of people, influences and ideas. Of course not all of them are *good* influences and ideas, but that's city life too. The point is, we do things together. Increasingly, this includes the way we grow our own food.

What is a community garden?

A community garden is not just about vegetables. It can be a farm, a playground, a school, a temple, a gym, a stage, a refuge, a wildlife habitat and more—all on the same day. At best it derives its strength from and serves as a model for the community around it. Community gardens teach and celebrate values we cherish, including cooperation, volunteering, appreciation for diversity and ecological awareness.

Some of the most inspirational ones I've seen have been in the neighborhoods that needed them most. At the Hastings Folk Garden in Vancouver's Downtown Eastside, ground zero for the city's social issues of homelessness, addiction, prostitution and crime, a single city lot was turned into an organic food garden. Residents of the neighborhood did much of the heavy work. Some didn't have homes themselves, which may be why the site turned into a farm that resembled an outdoor living room. All kinds of neighborhood people would drop in. Nurses would visit on breaks from the Insite safe injection clinic two doors away, the only legal facility in North America where addicts can use heroin, under medical supervision. Sometimes sex-trade workers would stroll in to pick a few raspberries off the vine, perhaps

Inner city herb harvest.

the only fresh organic food they would eat that day. Others would come in just to sit for twenty quiet minutes away from the chaos of the street. Urban agriculture is all about the food, but it can also be about much more than that.

And one for all

One of the shortest routes from passive consumer to active food-system designer is through the community garden.

Sometimes I get asked to speak to a group of neighbors wondering whether they have it in them to start and run a community garden. The answer is usually yes, but not always. I remind them that community gardens don't just sprout and grow out of good intentions. They take a lot of cooperation, dedication and plain hard work. Which means not just one or two keeners but a strong group of people, the more the better.

I make it a point to remind them, "The most important word in community gardening is the first one." But sometimes I screw up the first/second word thing, confusing myself along with the audience, so I'll add this to mean the same thing: "Community gardens grow community." By that I mean they make people and communities healthier, more socially aware and more ecologically engaged. They also grow food where people live, which is the aim of urban agriculture.

Farm friendly

Some cities are community garden-friendly, while other treat them like uninvited guests. Montreal falls into the accepting category. The city's first community garden, planted in 1975, was created when a group of immigrant residents asked if they could cultivate a neighborhood lot left empty by a fire. Fortunately for them the city official put onto the file was from the horticulture department, a garden person. He wasn't sure it would work, but was impressed with their enthusiasm and went along on good faith. When it succeeded, and the neighborhood was revitalized, bringing a diversity of residents together for the first time, the idea spread to other parts of the city.

Montreal now has some of the most supportive policies for urban agriculture in North America. It has an estimated ten thousand community gardeners. All city residents receive a notice with their electricity bill asking if they're interested in joining a nearby garden. Zoning regulations protect food-growing spaces. The city pays for *animateurs* to explain growing techniques to beginners.

So if your own city official gives you the runaround when you ask to use some unproductive city land to grow food, have them understand it's not a new or crazy idea. You might even mention what happened to that horticulturalist in Montreal: he went on to become mayor. Naturally it never hurts to have friends in high places, but it was a citizen-led effort that made the city an example for others to follow.

On the other hand, Montreal is based more on the allotment style of community gardening. Also popular in Europe, this is often a city-managed operation in which the gardeners pay a small fee each year in return for a numbered plot they are free to tend as they like, within the regulations. Allotment gardens work well to get many people on the land, with the city or whomever manages the facility taking care of much of the work.

A more community-oriented community garden is one the members manage themselves. Often they're involved in creating, planning, designing and building the garden. A city using this model usually has lower numbers of total gardeners. But it also usually gains in community development as the gardeners create their own sense of social harmony and civic engagement.

You can't automatically say one is better than the other, as both have their merits. Quantity and quality are both desirable aspects of the campaign to get more people growing more city food. But if I'm asked, I usually recommend quality. A community garden at its best can be the best thing about a community, and that's a tough claim for any allotment garden to match.

How to start a community garden

First, get a community.

It may be a community of two, but that's all right, you have to start somewhere, and two is twice as good as one. Even a determined individual can burn out in a flash if others don't soon catch on. If your project is at all viable for the area you propose, people will join in once they see the opportunity. The lure of the sun-warmed tomato should not be taken lightly.

If you have a garden space in mind, put up a poster nearby calling for a meeting to discuss it. Or if you're still looking, get the word out by free Craiglist postings, public messages on the community radio station, leafleting the neighborhood and papering the local bulletin boards. Try to target groups who may not normally get the news. To reach the percentage of intercultural community gardeners we needed for our downtown Vancouver project aimed at building a more inclusive society, we put out notices in five languages and made sure the ethnic press listed our public info sessions and community dialogue events where we had volunteer interpreters on hand. Sure enough, half the people who showed up were foreign-born, and many had never grown organic food before.

Next, get land. This can either be the hardest part of the process or it can go swimmingly. There's no one strategy for securing the various types of land held by various government agencies or private jurisdictions. One thing that helps is numbers: the more people you have asking, the easier it is to make your case that starting a community garden on a particular spot is a worthy idea.

When searching for a site, remember that sun is crucial. I know it sounds obvious, and it's been explained already earlier in this book, but it continues to surprise me how many people — including city officials — will seriously consider areas under thick canopies or in the shade of tall buildings.

You're obviously going to need water. If the site doesn't have a hookup already, you'll need to install it. This is where your good

Every unused lot is a potential farm.

contacts with the city can be put to use. A simple hookup, if it includes a backflow valve, can cost several thousand dollars. That's a lot for a small band of would-be growers, but peanuts for a city that does them all the time.

Plan your project with your newfound group. You might start with a name. Then determine your "mission statement," which is typically an explanation of your purpose. It can be brief or elaborate, but brief is better because it makes you crystallize what your group is really about, and can be useful to refer to in later years when new people and new situations require everyone to get their bearings. Here's what the Urban Farming nonprofit group from Detroit has declared they're all about: "Urban Farming's mission is to create an abundance of food for people in need by planting gardens on unused land and space while increasing diversity, educating youth, adults and seniors and providing an environmentally sustainable system to uplift communities." The intercultural community garden I worked with in Vancouver decided on this for their purpose: "To promote intercultural relations between Canadian-born and non-Canadian-born residents of the downtown peninsula of Vancouver through organic, community gardening in a supportive, healthy and inclusive environment."

Next do an asset check. What will you need to start and manage a garden? Begin by listing what you already have. If you do this with a group, you may be astonished to learn how resourceful your own neighbors can be. This is true both in terms of materials—you could dig your way to China with all the shovels lying around people's garages, and someone may also have a cousin with a backhoe—and in terms of skill and experience. Until you sit down together and someone asks, you may not know how many people can contribute their time as plumbers and carpenters and graphic designers and community organizers and landscape architects and lawyers and childminders and cooks and all the roles that add up to the social capital of a community.

Get funds. Community gardens can be launched and run on shoestring budgets, but you will eventually need some money—to buy shared tools or order a delivery of manure or plant some perimeter trees or get insurance (if required), and so on.

Community garden infrastructure costs can be kept low if you simply plant in the ground. Costs rise with more and better facilities. A fence can be expensive, in materials as well as in time if you're putting it up yourself. One estimate by city staff from North Vancouver uses a standard rate of $100 to $150 per linear meter. That's for a professionally constructed fence that will hold up for years. You can certainly do it cheaper yourself, and it may look that way, dismaying some, although a bit of wonky can add to the homemade charm. Maybe you don't need a fence — some gardeners prefer the open and welcoming look. Or, to provide at least a psychological barrier to thieves and a real one to dogs, they install closely planted shrubs or espalier fruit trees as a living fence.

Raised-bed planting boxes can add considerably to your start-up budget, depending on how many you need. The same North Vancouver estimate for boxes comes in at $15 to $35 per linear meter, or $25 per linear meter for a 30-cm-high installed box, again depending on materials chosen.

You may also need soil to fill up the first boxes or planting beds. Private companies where live I sell it for about $30 a yard, plus a delivery charge of an extra $50 to $75.

How many yards will you need? Multiply length by width by depth, then divide the total by 27. So for a box that's four feet by six feet and two feet high: $4 \times 6 \times 2 = 48$ cubic feet; divided by 27 it equals 1.7 cubic yards. A small pickup truck holds about a yard and a full-size pickup truck about two cubic yards.

Better together

The impact of a few neighbors getting together to talk about a better approach to food can seem slight, at first. In 1965 a Tokyo housewife thought the milk in the local stores wasn't that good, and expensive besides. She got some neighbors together to explore alternatives. They talked to others in turn, until the group was big enough to try buying in bulk directly from a dairy.

Thus began the Seikatsu Club cooperative. Today it has 22 million members, still mostly women.

The co-op's website says Seikatsu Club members, "with the cooperation of producers, refused to remain as passive consumers who buy appealing goods one by one in the market, and we at SC are now creating food and other essential goods with a concern for safety for human health and the environment." In 1989 the club won the Honorary Right Livelihood Award, the "alternative Nobel Prize," for being an "alternative economic activity against industrial society's prioritization of efficiency."

The fundamental principles of the SC are:

- Create a new lifestyle in order to protect environment and health. Stop passive and resource-wasteful lifestyles based on commercialism.
- Abolish differentials and discrimination. Realizing that "prosperity" based on the sacrifice of other people both in and outside of the country should not be pardoned, SC promotes and encourages fair trade.
- Establish autonomy of people. Stop following state control or an induction of commercial and industrial enterprises, but make every effort to create a community of autonomy and cooperation through our basic daily activities of collective purchase.
- Enable women, who are the majority of members, to be independent. Today's highly industrialized society pushed women and local communities into subordinate and decentralized positions. We are not only criticizing and confront-

FOURTEEN REASONS TO START A COMMUNITY GARDEN

1. Get neighbors together.
2. Learn/teach organic gardening.
3. Create or improve green spaces.
4. Cut crime.
5. Build economic activities.
6. Lower family food budgets.
7. Encourage self-reliance.
8. Enhance food democracy.
9. Reduce "food miles."
10. Increase biodiversity.
11. Reduce storm-water runoff.
12. Support urban nature.
13. Promote volunteering.
14. Reintroduce the commons.

ing the situation, but are proposing to create a new lifestyle and alternative work.

Seikatsu means "life," and reflects the guiding philosophy that there's more to it than money. The co-op refuses to buy genetically engineered foods, has a campaign to reduce Japan's ridiculous over-packaging habits and, through an affiliated network, has elected 141 members to local assemblies. It also has a fund to help new workers' collectives such as bakeries and recycling centers. In 1993 it launched a campaign to improve Japan's food self-sufficiency.

This is mentioned as a potential source of inspiration to start your own neighborhood conversations, perhaps beginning with food and how it is grown. And to point out that nothing happens until someone, maybe you, starts it. A simple glass of milk, a short row of carrots, an empty city lot spotted by a group of neighborhood growers — anything can happen when the seed of a good idea gets nurtured.

City politics, farm politics

If you thought growing food was a dirty business, wait until you get into the politics of trying to get support for growing food.

Cities are reluctant to devote land for food production. Why? Often because it's new, and policymakers, from civil "servants" to elected officials, know they're more likely to get burned than rewarded for backing anything new. Also because land use is one of the only significant decisions cities get to make these days, and they're under pressure from a lot of directions.

Food democracy advocates have not to date been one of the bigger players in pushing policy, but that may change as the global food system teeters. Vancouver is as well-connected as any place to the world's trading streams, but in an emergency it would have three days of food on which to get by. When we talk about "food security" we often think we're talking about the poor, such as the

800,000 Canadians who now visit food banks each month. The truth is we're all food-insecure—another reason why growing more local food is not just a feel-good movement but sound public policy.

In economic downturns, government agencies or private owners may be willing to lease land to people who want to grow food. The history of community gardening in North America is a series of booms and busts related to government support. Whenever there's a crisis and residents are faced with the problem of getting food, governments have encouraged public growing. Faced with the Panic of the 1890s and the Depression of the 1930s, as well as

Walk This Way

Examples & Inspiration

The Homeless Garden Project aims to solve two problems with one method: farming. We know homelessness is often caused by joblessness, so the Homeless Garden Project in Santa Cruz, California, helps people learn new skills, including self-confidence, by growing food and flowers. The project runs a CSA farm and a women's organic flower enterprise, while teaching youth and other groups. From its newsletter: "'Nobody wants to hire a single mom on welfare at age 50 with only a high school diploma,' can become, 'Well, here I am, one year later, I am the top propagator and in charge of the greenhouse. I propagate many different kinds of plants, pull orders, and help customers...' Both those statements were made by one of our graduates, the second one referring to her new job at a local nursery." The project just celebrated its twentieth anniversary.

— homelessgardenproject.org —

World War I and World War II, governments smartly got behind city farming. But each time, once the crisis ended, so did the official support, and the gardens were paved over for buildings, parking lots, whatever.

The problem with this reactive approach is it means you keep having to start all over again, only with a dwindling land supply. And it doesn't support good farming practices that maintain a steady supply of food. Growing healthy soil involves years of commitment by people who develop an affinity for the place. If you know your farm can be snatched away with the next economic upturn, you're hardly encouraged to develop the kind of intimate relationship with the land that living soil requires.

No matter how friendly and food-conscious they may appear, it's difficult to trust your politicians on this. Municipal politics is largely a money game, and cities never have enough, so the lure of cash-flinging developers and pressures from competing and perhaps more influential groups are often too much to endure. Better to get everyone on all sides to agree, now, that protecting city land for food is crucial to the city's future, and to get that commitment written into law.

City governments aren't the only bodies that need encouragement. State/provincial and federal governments should offer comprehensive support for urban agriculture in planning, education, marketing, distribution and funding that can reduce the inefficiencies of each city having to invent its own wheel. Agriculture at the larger government level has been long considered a rural, not urban, concern, but that way of thinking is out of date.

Why bother, the city/regional/federal politician might ask? Because urban farming is a good idea not just for the food. Farms absorb more rainwater and capture more carbon dioxide than lawns or empty land. More local farmers means more people involved in healthier work growing healthier food, both reducing the budget for health care. Urban farms can also cut the waste management budget, diverting some of the estimated 40 percent

THIRTEEN QUESTIONS TO ASK YOUR POLITICIANS DURING THE NEXT ELECTION

1. Do you agree food is a human right?

2. Why don't we have zoning to allow agriculture in all parts of the city if existing laws can cover nuisances?

3. Should growing food be included in all community visioning and land use planning?

4. Do you support an urban food-grower's co-op to get the city and farmers working together on needs and services?

5. What percent of the total property tax intake should be reserved for the local food system?

6. Should property taxes be lower for any land used to grow food?

7. How would you improve the institutional buying of local food?

8. Will you agree to mandate a minimum number of community garden plots per population (such as ten plots per thousand residents in each neighborhood)?

9. Will you back an usufruct law allowing growers to plant unused land?

10. What will you do to encourage a land trust for urban farms?

11. What plans do you have to create public spaces devoted to urban food such as farm demonstration sites, teaching orchards and festival/celebration areas?

12. What will you do to enhance edible landscaping?

13. Would you back a facility for urban farmers to share processing, marketing and selling food year-round?

of typical landfill trash that could be composted. Integrate waste sensibly and you can even get energy from it, burning methane to heat greenhouses to grow more food year-round.

Can it happen? It is already. San Francisco Mayor Gavin Newsom issued an executive directive in 2009 to reshape how San Franciscans think about food. "Urban agriculture is about far more than growing vegetables on an empty lot," he told the *San Francisco Chronicle*. "It's about revitalizing and transforming unused public spaces, connecting city residents with their neighborhoods in a new way and promoting healthier eating and living for everyone." Newsom's sixteen mandatory actions included requiring all city departments to audit unused spaces such as empty lots and rooftops to find sites suitable for farming. All city agencies purchasing food were told to buy healthy, locally produced goods wherever possible, and the parks department was told to help people gain access to tools and supplies to grow more city food.

Not to be outdone by some California upstart, Seattle declared 2010 the Year of Urban Agriculture. Backing up the niceties were actual policies clarifying the legal definitions of urban agricultural terms, expanding opportunities for community gardens and farms in all zones and raising the number of chickens permitted per household from three to eight.

TAKE HOME MESSAGE

It takes food to grow a village.

CHAPTER 8

SPEAK FOR THE TREES
UP WITH PUBLIC ORCHARDS

When we envision land and what might be grown on it, we often think in 2-D. The soil, the boundaries, the sum of the flat area in square feet or meters. Which is fine, for a start, but don't forget to look up. You live in a 3-D world, so let your imagination soar skyward. Think of how to maximize your growing space with shrubs and climbing vines and trees.

Unlike vegetable crops, which typically need replanting to start all over again each spring, these living food factories can be planted once to produce for generations. There may still be some care involved, such as pruning or soil fertility boosting, but the main task is also the most rewarding: harvesting the fruit. Surprising, this job is regularly ignored, at least when it comes to public fruit trees. People will step around the dropped fruit of a ripe tree on their way to the supermarket to buy food. It's a sign of how city living has dulled our common senses—and a suggestion that consciously growing food through urban agriculture can sharpen them back up.

Harvesting pears is half the fun.

TreePeople

The TreePeople group got its start in Los Angeles in 1970 when a fifteen-year-old summer camper learned that city smog was killing the trees around his group's mountain retreat. He organized fellow campers to plant a parking lot with air-purifying trees. The seeds of that idea sprouted into TreePeople, one of the most successful environmental groups in the state.

In 1981 when city officials were worried about air pollution affecting athletes at the upcoming 1984 Olympic Games, they estimated that one million additional trees would be needed to make a difference—but lamented the fact they didn't have the twenty years and $200 million it would take to plant them. So TreePeople offered to do it for free. With the help of a lot of people, including celebrities, it planted its one-millionth tree four days before the opening ceremonies.

Today TreePeople is looking at LA's environmental problems from the perspective of an urban forest, using trees in the redesign of neighborhoods to conserve water and reduce storm-water run-off. It also supports a growing fruit tree campaign, offering trees and training to people in low-income neighborhoods who might otherwise have few opportunities to get fresh, healthy, organic produce.

When I visited it was hard not to be envious of the range of fruit trees they can grow in that near-constant sunshine. But it made sense. Southern California used to be filled with orchards, before they were chopped down in the great sprawl. It was encouraging to see how they are being brought back, this time right in the neighborhoods, almost as if to recreate the old enticement posters for the California dream that featured lucky residents picking oranges through the kitchen window for the breakfast table.

Tree City

Tree City was launched in Vancouver in 2005 by a group of environmental activists determined to "help people and trees grow together," mostly by getting people to plant and care for the urban forest, whether it was in their yards, streets, parks, schools or elsewhere. Behind it was the notion that city residents needed to be more engaged in the ecological health of their own communities, and trees were a good way to get them there.

Every culture below the tundra has its legends and mythologies in which trees play a crucial role. Religions too. Christians have the forbidden fruit of the apple tree (which some say would more likely have been a quince) and Buddhists have the Bodhi tree—*Ficus religiosa*, a member of the fig family—under which the Buddha sat with a vow to stay until he achieved enlightenment.

SIX GOOD THINGS ABOUT FRUIT TREES

1. Fruit.
2. Visual appeal in all stages from bloom to harvest to dormancy.
3. They're a living laboratory for hands-on science experiments such as grafting.
4. They need less maintenance than vegetable crops.
5. Shade, fragrance, screening, wood.
6. They remind us we all live in an urban forest.

Trees are a universal language that can help drive an urban agriculture project, especially in a city like Vancouver where more than half the population speaks a mother tongue other than English as their mother tongue. Fruit trees have proven especially popular as a topic for workshops on tree care. People from every part of the world get it when it comes to beautiful, graceful, living things that produce armloads of sweet things to eat. Our explanations on organic fruit tree selection or apple grafting are done in English, but some people invariably show up to learn by watching. Consider fruit trees an ally if you ever need to win over hearts and minds in your urban neighborhood.

How to plant a tree

If you want a community orchard that does your community proud, be sure to start with quality trees.

People spend more time studying a lunch menu than they do a garden center tree that may live with them for decades. Don't rush this decision. Take the time you need to make sure you get the right tree for the right place. People buy trees all the time without doing the first calculation to determine if the mature tree will even fit where they intend to plant it.

Check the trees at the garden center for healthy growth, good branch structure, thick trunks with taper and straight roots that begin in the uppermost two inches of soil. If the one you're after doesn't pass muster, reject it. Rather than spend years trying to correct a nursery's problems, insist from the start on quality trees. If enough people do, eventually they'll get the point.

If you couldn't inspect the roots in the garden store, do it just before you plant. Any circling roots should be straightened out or cut. If left to grow in the same direction, they may thicken and eventually strangle the tree.

Dig a hole three times as wide but no deeper than the root ball or tree pot with a firm, flat bottom to prevent sinking. One of the most common mistakes people make is to plant too deeply. Trees absorb most of their water and oxygen from roots growing near the soil surface, so planting too deeply can result in stunted growth or suffocation. Lay a long-handled shovel across the open hole to determine where the soil surface will be, then make sure the tree's trunk flare—the part where it spreads out to meet the uppermost roots—is above it.

Backfill with soil removed from the hole. You don't need to add anything like bone meal or extra fertilizer—in fact it may only discourage roots from growing beyond the perimeter of the hole. Press down to remove any large air pockets. Build a four-inch-high berm around the perimeter to help collect water, then irrigate well.

Staking may be necessary, depending on the tree size and type. Some trees, such as apples on the popular M9 dwarf rootstock, need staking for their entire lifetimes since their root structures may not be strong enough to keep a fruit-laden canopy upright.

Mulch out to the berm with organic material such as leaf litter, shredded bark or wood chips. This helps conserve soil moisture, prevents weeds from competing for water and nutrients, and keeps all but the most maniacal landscrapers with their weed-eaters away from the trunk. Don't let the mulch come in contact with the trunk: the constant moisture could rot the bark and invite disease.

Irrigation is critical for the tree, especially in its first growing season. One to three deep waterings per week should be enough, but monitor in dry weather to be sure—drooping leaves beginning at the branch tips are tree language for "I'm thirsty."

Pruning strategies depend on the species. If you're unsure where and when to cut, get a book, do a net search or ask an experienced arborist. It helps to determine a structure to maximize fruit production before you start hacking away. Some fruit trees do best with a central leader—think of a Christmas tree—while others may be more prolific with a vase-like open center. Keep in mind that your goal is to get as many branches as possible holding their sun-collecting leaves up to the sunlight.

Big fig

You can have your fruit and other things too. With the growing selection of dwarf fruit varieties available these days, even a small city space can be used to grow a diverse selection of edibles.

Umberto Garbuio is an ace gardener I know in Burnaby, bordering Vancouver. Originally from Italy, he likes food, big surprise, but also flowers—his basement is crammed with ribbons and trophies from fuchsia-growing competitions. What to do? Both. Garbuio grows flowers throughout his property in the kind of eye-catching displays that make pedestrians stop and stare, but he also grows plenty of food, including tree fruits. Grape vines stretch along the backyard fence, kiwis grow against the house, and in the back, beside and along and on top of the garage, is the largest fig tree in Canada.

Umberto Garbuio and the biggest fig tree in Canada.

At least Garbuio believes it is the largest. And it sounds impressive when you learn he can collect 250 pounds of Italian honey figs in a single crop, but the biggest in the country? A local newspaper once printed the claim, and Garbuio was soon contacted by rivals. "Originally they come here from Turkey, Italy, Portugal, Greece, so they grow figs too. They come to see my tree," he explained. "They think maybe theirs is bigger. And what happens? They all go home saying mine is the biggest. One man, from Turkey, he shook his head. He told me he thought he had a big tree before, but now he realizes, compared to mine his is just a branch."

I asked Garbuio for advice on growing production-level fruit. For figs, he said, which are Mediterranean and need plenty of heat to produce the sweetest fruit, location is key. That's why he grows his beside the garage, a big white-painted structure that absorbs and radiates heat from the sun. Then there's pruning. It's not a difficult task, but you need to know that figs fruit on last year's wood, so if you blithely trim the ends off your branches every year, don't be surprised if your trees continually put out lots of leaves but never any fruit.

Fruit for all

The campaign to get more public fruit into public places is one of those ideas that everybody loves but few actually work to see

Trees bring people together.

through. It's not enough to hope for it, or if you're a politician to say it's a grand idea. You still need to think through the how, where and by whom the trees will be planted and cared for.

Much of your city's urban forest will be managed by city arborists. They probably haven't have been trained to deal particularly with fruit trees, but as tree people, and eaters, they may well be amenable to the idea. The problem is more with city administrators. Public officials are often reluctant to plant public fruit, and not without reason: it will lead to increased complaints that they'll have to handle. People will rail about fallen fruit, bears, bees, wasps, rodents, birds and more. If it's about street trees, they'll swear a bushel of rotten fruit will fall on their car, and if it's

Walk This Way

Examples & Inspiration

West Oakland was known more for poverty and pollution than for fresh food in 2001, when resident Willow Rosenthal donated the use of a plot of land to grow some. Thus began City Slicker Farms, a volunteer group determined to get the area's empty lots into food production. Today the group helps residents manage seven community market farms, over a hundred backyard gardens, a weekly farm stand and a greenhouse, and runs urban farming education programs. In November 2010, it won a grant of $4 million from a California voter initiative to reserve $5.4 billion in bonds for environmental projects. It will use the grant to buy land for a new farm.

— **cityslickerfarms.org** —

about sidewalk trees they'll be convinced that somebody will slip on a slimy pit and break their neck.

All of which is possible, but none of which is enough to take fruit trees off the city list. After all, handling problems between trees and people is what cities do. It's why we have professional arborists on the city payroll. Shade trees are defining features in many cities around the world; they make living in crowded urban areas tolerable. But they're also a nuisance. They drop leaves that clog storm drains, attract insects such as aphids that excrete sticky goo on cars, lift and crack sidewalks, and even kill people when they collapse. None of these drawbacks are considered grave enough to eliminate trees from our cities, and fruit trees should be seen no differently—except that they may have the advantage of encouraging more citizen participation in caring for their urban forest.

This is the key to making public fruit work—engaging the public from the start. Many of the worries about maintenance can be handled by enthusiastic volunteers, such as the Citizen Pruners licensed to help care for New York City's trees or the Tree Tenders trained by the Pennsylvania Horticultural Society's Philadelphia Green program. If neighbors are involved in selecting, planting and caring for the fruit trees in their area, chances are they'll also be involved in swooping up all the fruit before it causes any problems.

Community orchards

Community orchards can be neighborhood builders for all the reasons described in the last chapter on community gardens. For certain people and places, community orchards may be even better.

Trees offer an opportunity to engage in physical outdoor activity better suited to some, including those less bendable such as seniors and others unable or unwilling to do the digging and weeding grunt work required to grow vegetables.

Community orchards can offer quiet contemplation, casual recreation including jogging and dog walking, pleasant surroundings for picnickers and opportunities for local festivities. The harvested fruit can go to the volunteers who help tend the orchard and/or to local food banks, schools or community kitchens.

The English are keener than most on the beauty and natural value of orchards. Once widespread throughout the British islands, fruit trees have been disappearing at an alarming clip. Not long ago every farm or home with enough space had its own collection of fruit trees. New housing developments and cheap fruit imports from abroad have wiped out many of the small and large orchards. One study reports England losing 60 percent of its orchards since 1960. So tree lovers are now looking for community-based opportunities to preserve them.

Community orchards can reprise the role of the countryside woods of the past. They can become a focal point for a neighborhood, an "open-air village hall" in the words of the UK group Common Ground, which promotes school orchards, city orchards, museum orchards, hospital orchards and factory orchards. "Community Orchards help to revive an interest in fruit growing, provide a way of sharing knowledge and horticultural skills and stimulate us into growing food for ourselves again." Check out their website for info, descriptions and advice on community orchards (commonground.org.uk).

Whose fruit?

People considering community orchards often wonder how the fruit should be distributed. Every community orchard decides what to do with its own harvest. Since it's not a commercial orchard under economic pressure to make a profit every season, production can be far less stressful. The easiest distribution method is probably to let those who do the work take home the fruit. This can be done by agreeing beforehand on which individual will get the fruit from which tree, but because of yield variances between

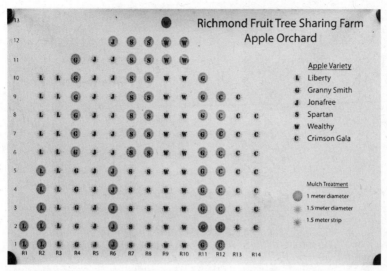

Planting plan for a public orchard.

species and even with the same tree in different years, you may decide instead to share the harvest communally among all those who help in the orchard. It sounds like it could get complicated, but in the orchard in my community garden, we just spread the haul out during a monthly work party and invite people to take some home. Some only want a couple of apples, some take them by the bagful, but everyone seems to leave happy.

This is a planting plan for a community orchard in Richmond next to Vancouver. The 139 heritage apple trees on M7A rootstock were placed 16 feet apart in rows 18 feet apart. Kent Mullinex, an educator and orchardist helping the Richmond Fruit Tree Sharing Farm growers, says he now wishes they had planted more densely, but adds, it's all an experiment. Among the things this orchard is contributing, besides public apples, is public information. Tests are being conducted on optimum mulching levels for growth and to determine the effectiveness of planting on mounds to rise above the area's high water table.

Trees in modern orchards using espalier methods on dwarf rootstock can be spaced as little as two feet apart. This is great for maintenance and production, and is the style I often recommend

A lot of fruit can be grown in little space using the espalier method.

to homegrowers since fruit is the main point and they typically don't live on large estates. You can grow a large variety and amount of tasty apples in the space of a driveway.

But in the bigger picture of public spaces, some consider the landscape a poorer place for its loss of large fruit trees on standard rootstock. Using the example of trees traditionally planted in England, cider apples were typically spaced 35 feet apart. Cherry trees were placed 48 feet apart and some varieties such as Perry pears, which can live more than 300 years, were planted a full 60 feet apart. They would eventually grow together into magical spaces of gnarled old wood under luminous green canopies and dangling fruit.

This is an entirely different approach to spatial potential and long-term planning than we may be used in the cities, but if you've got the room, the results can pay off for generations to come. Think of keeping at least one of these majestic structures to span the distance from earth to the heavens in a way that draws the eye and lifts the spirit. Even a lone standard tree can support climbing kids and shade-lounging couples and a rope-tire swing and still provide apples by the bushel.

Glean this

You don't need to plant an orchard to get a city full of fruit just waiting to be harvested. A surprising number of residential tree owners never collect the harvest from their own trees. Maybe they lost the ladder or they didn't plant the tree and aren't sure what that pear-shaped thing might be. Or maybe they just don't care, although they do recognize waste when they see it, and therefore feel badly enough about the whole thing to agree to let others use the fruit. A number of cities have evolved volunteer groups to glean otherwise neglected harvests. Toronto's Not Far From the Tree organization picked 20,000 pounds of cherries, plums, apples, crab apples, pears, grapes, ginko nuts and more in 2010. The harvest was divided into thirds: one third to the tree owner, one third to the volunteer harvesters and one third to community organizations.

Shrub love

We're already inundated with shrubbery in our cities. Shrubbery to hide things, shrubbery to carve into blobs or lollipops, shrubbery that's there just because it's always been there. Much of it is planted without thought or devotion, and accordingly is not loved by anyone. Professional designers and landscapers are forever inserting shrubbery into places so it can be ignored until the weekly mow-and-blow crew shows up to give it a trim.

Here's a way to have your shrubbery stand out: make it edible. Check out the genus *Vaccinium* for a long list of interesting-in-all-seasons shrubs that also offer some fantastic taste delights: blueberry, cranberry, lingonberry, huckleberry, and the list goes on.

The Renfrew/Collingwood Food Security Institute in Vancouver planted a Native Berry Trail along a public route to feed people's heads as well as bellies. The project demonstrates the beauty of native plants, emphasizing this point with salmonberries, wild raspberries, gooseberries, Oregon grape and others. There's nothing quite like flavor to drive a lesson home.

TAKE HOME MESSAGE

Eat the urban forest.

CHAPTER 9

NEW URBAN FARMS
BIG-ISH IS BETTER-ISH

Urban agriculture in North America is changing. The pace of this change is so rapid it's hard to know where it'll be even a few years from now. Like they say about the new green roof industry in North America: we're building this ship at sea.

But here's a prediction anyway: urban agriculture will move ahead in all directions. Individuals in residential yards and part-time farmers in shared spaces will grow in number and intensity as food prices and health concerns rise. More people will grow more food, in ways that might not be obvious now. Perhaps most noticeable will be bigger city farms managed by full-time farmers. These will appear in empty lots and idle tracts of government land, in parks and industrial areas, on rooftops and around housing complexes, around schools and hospitals and prisons, in greenhouses and indoor facilities. These bigger farms may be government-managed, cooperative ventures, land trust setups, social ventures, entrepreneurial projects or who-knows-what?

Land matters

Ramping up urban agriculture from our present stage to larger farms involves some of the same barriers we have seen all along. Chief among them is land and who owns it. Right? Well, not exactly. Who *owns* it may be less important than who gets to *use* it, and for how long. Why get stuck on property when it's an ephemeral concept, and on one level not really that useful since we're all just passing through anyway. The key question is land use, which involves tenure.

Tenure does not come into conversations about urban agriculture as often as one might expect. In my city, where any suggestion to use even a small portion of the public bounty is contested (remember the angry rich folks in the intro), growers have tended to accept any offer of farm space, even when it's tenuous. When the market for new condo projects hit a rut, developers found they had empty lots on their hands. But they still had to pay hefty property taxes — unless they could say the land was being used as a green space, in which case the taxes were cheap. So in some places they offered the land to community gardeners. The growers often didn't realize the extent of the savings because no one bothered to ask. When it came to a choice between land or nothing, that gift horse's mouth seemed fine. Maybe it still is fine. I'm never sure

SEVEN REASONS TO SCALE UP

1. Improve degraded neighborhoods.
2. Create green jobs.
3. Reduce food miles.
4. Get farmers and consumers together.
5. Reduce storm-water runoff.
6. Help re-build the local food system.
7. Support regional processing, distribution and marketing.

Even the suburbs become interesting when farms are included.

what to recommend when one of these deals comes up, especially after learning that speculators can save millions through lower tax rates while contributing little to the gardens beyond perhaps adding a few temporary planting beds. Put another way, money that's actually ours, as tax revenue, stays in the developers' pockets. Yes, growers do get access to land, but only until the market opportunities rise. That's not a sound strategy for building a healthy farm or strengthening a community's capacity to create its own lasting food solutions.

Around Vancouver, land is so expensive that no prospective farmer with a calculator can figure out how to grow enough food to pay off a mortgage. At least not when their food has to compete in price with supermarket fare that may 1) be imported from countries where farmworkers earn little, 2) come from factory farms that can sell their crops at pennies above production costs while counting on huge volumes to make it add up, and 3) entice customers into the store with loss-leaders on fresh produce. The challenges are overwhelming for a small farmer with a crippling mortgage, which is why alternative land models such as co-ops, land trusts and publicly funded farms are seen as the answer.

This is not just a local matter. The question of land and who gets to work it is a concern as big as the world. Farmers everywhere are being pushed off the land as rich countries, corporations and profiteers try to take care of their own. The way to resist is to involve the only player big enough to stand up to moneyed interests: all of us, together, through our governments. Elected officials must be held to account so they'll stand up for us, growers and consumers, together. The strategy isn't a mystery. It's already been described by the International Assessment of Agricultural Knowledge, Science and Technology for Development (IAASTD), a UN- and World Bank-funded study by more than 400 scientists in 120 countries: "It is time to fundamentally rethink the role of agricultural knowledge, science and technology in achieving equitable development and sustainability. The focus must turn to the needs of small farms in diverse ecosystems and to areas with the greatest needs."

Are your politicians slow to get that point? Remind them what happened in Madagascar when the government there cut a deal to sell (actually lease for 99 years) *half* of the country's arable land to the South Korean corporation Daewoo. The people of Madagascar chased the president out of the palace.

Where's the mob of angry citizens when you need them? A similar landgrab may be happening right here in North America, only we haven't recognized it yet. According to Canada's National Farmers Union:

> "The farm model of the past 100 years (numerous, relatively stable and autonomous family farm operations interdependent with, and interlinked to, communities) is being dismantled at an accelerating rate. We may be on the verge of a new system wherein those who work the land do not own it, a situation that would look familiar and comforting to a thirteenth-century lord."

You're so special

Let's take the positive view that the tectonic changes now rumbling beneath us are going to shift things in our favor. Cooperation is never more valuable than at the dawn of a new era when new standards are being established. A shared view of how urban agriculture can fit into and around cities would allow specialization according to the optimal local conditions. Farmers could raise food as their microclimate, soil conditions, transportation logistics and other factors support. It turns out those horizon-reaching rural spreads aren't needed for the kind of intensive operations urban agriculture is all about. Crannies, nooks and patches, which are found in every city are ideal. The end of one street might have sandy soil well suited to carrots. A peach orchard might be located in a wind-protected ravine that soaks up lots of sun. Rolling pastureland on the outskirts could be devoted to goats or sheep or cows. And so on. This is where our notions of the city as a giant farm begin to take shape. With more farmers in the conversation from the start, cooperating, a comprehensive picture may emerge that works to feed the city, or at least as much of it as possible, while ensuring that the farmers inside and beyond get to do their work at a fair wage.

New family, new family farm

So much dire news, you'd wonder why anyone would consider a future as a farmer. It's great that concerts with Farm Aid stalwarts like Willie Nelson raise funds for victims of the corporate hurricane blowing through rural communities, but all that doom and gloom might leave you thinking the family farm is dead.

It isn't dead, it's hanging on, but not by much. Corporations and banks own more of it every year. In Canada, farmers now take on $23 in debt for each dollar they earn. That's a huge burden for anyone, and especially for farmers facing an income crisis with profitable years as rare as hen's teeth. Most are able to carry on only with the help of off-farm income.

Then there's the concern about aging farmers. The average farmer in the US is said to be 57 years old. That might add up to something even older in regular, non-farmer years—the work can be hard on the body. On the other hand, that statistic may be skewed by the fact that farms often remain in the parents' name even when the work is taken over by the children. But it's also true that the children of many farmers look at all the effort, and the payoff, then opt for more attractive employment opportunities in growth industries such as pet grooming and prison management.

This is again a place where the city has a role, and it's an important one: to save the family farmer. It may involve a tweaking of the definition, but it's probably high time for that. If our idea of the meaning of the farm is in flux, so is our concept of the family.

One of the most uplifting trends on the food democracy scene today is the number of young North Americans eager to go back to the farm. (That's "back" in the wider sense of human history; in many cases they're coming from entirely urban backgrounds.) Youth getting seriously into something can change the culture, the sea in which society, business, manners, the arts and much more float. Better still, many of these aspiring farmers are into it as a way to do right by the planet. They're looking at organic practices, agro-ecology and integrating farms into healthy local economies. So city farmers might have something to say about saving the family farm, not just for the farmers but for everyone. This new trend is unlike the 1960s when counter-culture types fled the cities to go "back to the land." In the 2010s, they're realizing the "land" is under their feet—in the cities where they live.

Super non-store

The rise of farmers' markets is a fast-growing trend, but not exactly new. Settlers brought the tradition of public markets to North America from Europe as far back as the seventeenth century. Urban customers used these first markets as their primary sources of fresh produce, dairy, meat, fish and poultry.

Why they ever fell out of favor, and are only recently gaining such popularity, is a longer story that won't be told here. It's enough to say, farmers' markets: good; present system in which produce travels an average 1,500 miles before it is consumed: madness.

Some customers are shocked when they see the prices at a farmers' market. It's true, they can be high. Why pay four dollars for a handful of green beans when they're on sale for less than half that amount at the supermarket? Partly because a second, more pleasant shock may come with the taste. Vegetables start losing flavor once they're picked, so imagine the difference between just-harvested beans and something that had to be shipped or flown and trucked halfway around the planet.

Of course, if price is the only factor, you could go with the instant noodles I had for lunch. (Why? So you don't have to.) They cost 80 cents. The package listed 53 ingredients. The last one was "artificial flavor."

I survived the experience. Although I think I would be feeling better about myself and my role as a global citizen right now if I'd eaten real food. But what about the price issue? Won't cheaper food always win in the end? Hugh Joseph of the New Entry Sustainable Farming Project at Tufts University in Massachusetts

FIVE REASONS TO SELL AT A FARMERS' MARKET

1. Minimum capital needed to get started.
2. Share the savings from cutting out middlemen.
3. Enthusiastic customer base.
4. Market research is immediate through direct feedback and support.
5. Unsuccessful sales strategies can be quickly changed.

compared the U.S. government's "Thrifty Food Plan" to a version featuring local, sustainable food. The government plan costs $152 a month for one person. Joseph's community-friendly version costs $162 a month, not a huge difference, and would probably keep the participant alive longer. He achieved his results by striking from the government list such items as soda pop, luncheon meats and TV dinners, and adding more of the things that draw throngs to farmers' markets: vegetables.

Pocket markets

These smaller versions of farmers' markets offer a chance to expand the concept further, sometimes into neighborhoods considered "food deserts" because no supermarket will bother going there. In Vancouver pocket markets have been set up in various locations: the workplace lobbies of high-rise office towers, a low-income district downtown where the residents can spend their limited dollars at dozens of bars but almost no produce markets,

Farmers' markets [left] have already spawned a successful offshoot, the smaller pocket market [right].

street corners in prosperous residential neighborhoods, and even beside a popular bike route.

Guerrilla farms

The first guerrilla farm I saw was in a "borrowed" Vancouver lot in 2006. The following year it became a CSA venture. With more people catching on to the idea that they don't have to own land to grow food (remember our word of the day, *usufruct*), these clandestine operations are popping up like morels after a rain. They may not be big enough to make a dent in the local food economy yet, but they are important sources of fresh produce for people with limited options, and they can be used as learning laboratories where farmers develop their craft. Many of them get into it for political or environmental or personal lifestyle reasons, but if some start making decent money, more advanced and sophisticated operations will surely not be far behind.

Farm entrepreneurs

The growth of entrepreneur-farmers brings a glow to the hearts of people convinced that the only way urban agriculture is going to succeed is when farmers discover it can pay off. I'm not so sure myself, because I also see the need for society as a whole to support urban farming based on the understanding that the benefits we all get from having more growers in our cities cannot and should not be measured in sales dollars alone. There are innovative ways to ensure a good living for urban farmers that don't involve competing directly with the cheapest food in world history, but we can work on that one. For now, it's encouraging to see entrepreneurs getting into the game, bringing their hybrid of growing skills and gambling techniques together.

One admirable trait I find in the entrepreneurs is their endless creativity. They know thinking outside the box is good because it might result in a new method or product the market will love. So they're not bound by farming traditions that rely on the same-old to define how things are supposed to work. Rather than combines and silos, some start out with bicycles and empty roof spaces. The same sense of exploring all possibilities can influence the marketing and distribution side as well. Rather than deal with the same distribution agent everybody uses, city farmers are looking at local farmers' markets, direct sales to restaurants, farm gate sales, CSAs and so on. This is city thinking, a way of working within the constraints of local conditions while drawing on a diverse wealth of experiences to come up with new ideas.

Marketing and distribution are also areas where the public, through policy, can contribute. Many small farmers could grow a number of crops that aren't currently viable because the market for small producers is limited or uncertain. Vegetables, for instance, are typically bought by big distributors at a volume and consistency beyond the capacity of small farmers. Government regulations at present favor this sector of the global food system, even if quality and public health end up suffering. This is where the small farmer should be at an advantage: quality and freshness are two things consumers say they will support with their wallets. But there has to be a reliable marketing and distribution structure for the small farmer to have a chance. Vancouver is hoping to set one up with a year-round farmers' market facility that would serve as a processing, distribution, storage and education center celebrating local food.

Find a niche

Farmers are not just food producers but businesspeople who must sell their wares. So think of what to grow for certain types of customers, or products that might fill the desires of buyers who never knew they had them until you came along.

Arzeena Hamir, of the Richmond Urban Farmers, had a sweet deal going with a restaurant run by a chef who was mad for their French Breakfast radishes. Those are the long red ones with the white tip, but he only wanted them at lipstick size. He cooked them with the leaves intact for some fancy dish that must have sold for a decent price because he was willing to pay Hamir's group $15 a bundle.

Before you run to the garden store for radish seeds, Hamir also points out that restaurants may not be the gold mines some growers expect, despite the prices you see on their menus. Like everyone else these days, chefs are under pressure to cut costs. And they tend to prefer dealing with suppliers who can guarantee a consistent product. They can't afford to rely on someone who might not come through an hour before prep time.

Then there are flowers. People pay a lot for bouquets that come from far-off places using all kinds of dubious growing practices... so how about local flowers sold to the same people who say they'll pay extra for local food? Make them organic flowers and you'll have an even stronger sales pitch.

Medicine is a zillion dollar industry you might explore, challenging Big Pharma with your modest herbal therapy plants. Learn how to make teas and tinctures and you might be able to extend your market reach year-round by selling value-added crops.

You might also consider U-pick operations. City people love to take part in their own farm experience. Every strawberry or blueberry you sell is one less piece you have to pick, sort, package, display and distribute yourself.

People farmer — Will Allen

The new urban agriculture movement in North American is already growing champions, most of whom are uncelebrated beyond their local areas. One stands above the rest — literally, at six-foot-seven, with hands the size of catcher's mitts that he scoops into compost bins to hold up the wriggling cadres of worms he credits for fueling his "good food revolution."

Will Allen played pro basketball in Europe and in the old ABA, did corporate time in marketing with Proctor & Gamble, but found his true calling back on the farm. Growing food was

Will Allen leads a workshop at his Milwaukee headquarters.

in his blood, from childhood, and he took to it later in life with a passion fulsome enough to share. For two years he worked on his Milwaukee urban farm for profit, then when a friend suggested he help out a youth group at the same time, he says, "I kind of got sucked into this."

The organization he now heads, Growing Power, has ten farms in and around Milwaukee and Chicago. It had fifty-two employees at the end of 2010, and said he was planning to add fifty more in the coming year. He counts on the help of two thousand volunteers, supplies food for an estimated ten thousand people a year, and continues to train 17–24-year-olds in career skills while offering hands-on lessons to anyone who thinks there may be a future in urban agriculture. He says the organization works in seventy different ways to improve the food system, from education to advocacy, because "too many people just talk about how to fix the system. What we do best is inspire people to go into some kind of action."

I signed up for a weekend workshop at the Growing Power headquarters in Milwaukee. I'd heard enough about Allen to wonder how much of his act was hype, but he turned out to be readily

Growing Power demonstrates how to get a lot of food out of small spaces.

likable. He seems genuinely interested in turning more city folks into farmers — if they're willing to work — and having them spread the movement in turn. "None of the stuff we teach here is new. Actually we've picked up a lot of it from people who came to our workshops. So if you learn something, pass it on."

This sentiment may have been inspired by one of Allen's earliest funders, Heifer International, which turns aid recipients into donors by encouraging them to "pass on the gift" of a calf or seeds or training. Allen handed us a form called "Passing on the Gift — Community Food Systems from the Ground Up" that included a pledge that read: "In receiving this training, I agree to pass on the skills and knowledge I have acquired to another member of my community within 6 months."

The workshop sessions covered techniques such as growing sprouts for the market, building hoop houses, setting up aquaculture systems to raise fish and vegetables, and starting vermiculture worm compost systems. Growing Power composts more than a hundred thousand pounds of waste every week, reducing the amount that would otherwise get driven to Wisconsin and Illinois landfills by six million pounds a year. The combined food waste, farm waste, coffee grounds and brewery dregs get transformed into enough fertile worm castings to run his intense planting operations. You cannot walk anywhere in the Growing Power headquarters, even in the middle of winter, without constantly turning or ducking to avoid trays and hanging pots filled with greens.

Seventy aspiring farmers from around North America attended the same workshop. They were a mix of ages and races and genders and levels of experience, a snapshot of the diversity that will make up the urban agriculturalists of the future. There are longer courses spread out over several months that include more economic advice and the chance to work on a business plan, but a weekend offers a good look into some of the practical operations. With enough gumption, this may be all the ambitious grower needs to decide it's worth giving a shot.

The question running through a lot of people's minds at the workshop, and still through mine, is whether it can pay off. This is a big question, indeed, for urban agriculture. Some say it can, and are busy finding out whether they're right, by actually trying. In many cases, success at these early stages is being measured not by bank accounts but experiences. If the farmers are able to farm full-time, and at the end of the season tally everything up and decide they can do it again the following year, they're living the dream.

Will Allen's own story is inspirational, but also an anomaly. Your farm may not be able to emulate his two thousand volunteers (although you might be fortunate enough to attract a "crop mob," a roving mass of landless volunteers who show up en masse to help get 'er done...more info at cropmog.org). You also may not have as many friends in high places. Allen has been talking with the Clinton Global Initiative about expanding to South Africa, and he gets invited to eat at the White House where he chats with Michelle Obama about her own front-yard organic farm. He also gets funds from leading the workshops ($350 per person for the two days of lessons) and from lecturing and grants: the Kellogg Foundation gave him $400,000 and his MacArthur "genius award" was worth $500,000.

The Growing Power workshops provide figures to let people come to their own conclusions about economic viability. I didn't hear it mentioned, but another lesson might be taken from the fact of the organization itself, particularly in its hybrid approach. Cities are ecosystems where edge species, creatures such as crows and coyotes that straddle the wild and developed regions, learn how to work the margins and thrive. Maybe there's a lesson in there for new urban farmers. Allen raises food for the market while at the same time employing youth, providing workshops, advising on policy and giving public speeches. Farming is a constant process of thinking ahead to guess what new seeds or techniques might work next season. Some of the successful practitioners in the new urban agriculture may be the ones who figure out how to sell city folks on more than just food.

Will Allen himself encourages those who may still be dithering. "This is not a new kind of farming but it is a new kind of food system we're building and we need to have everybody involved. We can't have a sustainable society without a sustainable food system. This is not the time to talk. It's the time for action. I meet a lot of folks who want to meet to talk about urban agriculture. I go away and one year later they're still talking. There is no perfect time to start. You might start out a little raggedy, but you'll get better. You'll grow your technical skills as you grow your infrastructure. And don't think money is everything. It isn't. Passion is the thing that will drive you to success."

Co-op farmer — David Catzel

For word from a farm that looks like a farm, with a tractor and everything, I drove about an hour out of Vancouver to Aldergrove in the Fraser Valley to visit David Catzel at the Fraser Common Farm. The farm is a 21-acre collectively owned site. Five of the

David Catzel.

acres are cultivated, and the rest is left as natural riparian (streamside) areas and woodland. It started in the 1970s when the Community Alternatives Co-op bought land in the valley and in the city to try to link the two in a meaningful way. The business side has gone through a number of changes and partnerships, most recently selling at farmers' markets under the Glorious Organics Cooperative banner.

Maybe because it was near sunset, when all the crops and surrounding forests were touched golden, or maybe it was because Catzel's two adorable kids joined in to help guide the tour and coax me into trying the tastiest vegetables, but I didn't want to leave. How could city life compete with this? We talked about farms and owls and berries and the salmon that ran in their stream as recently as a couple of years ago, flopping up to die at their feet after spawning in a journey that probably took in a sizable portion of the globe.

Catzel did not come from farming roots. He started out in the city volunteering with the Environmental Youth Alliance, a nonprofit organization teaching career skills and urban greening techniques. Later he worked for them, which included a stint in Ecuador, and did an eight-month apprenticeship in organic growing on the Linnaea Farm on Cortez Island, a ferry ride away from Vancouver.

"I guess I came out of that experience feeling like a farmer, but a farmer with maybe far too high ideals in terms of my lightness of land. I came here and farmed for one year and swore I would never farm again."

But he did come back, perhaps even wiser for the added

experience in other jobs. I suggested more people were getting interested these days in knowing whether they can make a living growing food.

"Yeah, it's easy to make tons of money farming," he said, and laughed before going on to explain. "If you look at the highest prices of things at a farmers' market, you're paying for someone to make somewhere between $12 and $15 hour — if they're really efficient. We don't hire $8-an-hour workers. The differential between the top-paying salary and a first-year worker is $2. So we pay ourselves $12 and any new people get $10 and if they stick around it goes up fairly quickly. If you look at the prices at the farmers' market, that's the type of salary you're supporting. I've always wondered about putting it on a sliding scale that said: 'This is what you pay if you want us to earn $12 hour, here's what you pay if you want us to earn $20 hour.' You think it would work?"

Some people might have stopped reading at that $12 an hour.

"That's where the lifestyle part comes in. I go out and watch my kids eat kale off the plant and I can't really put a price on that. Just to go out in the field and have access to the food we have? It's a nice environment, there are plenty of good people around, we live here and work from home so I don't have much of a commute, I just walk out the door. The work is really rewarding and very diversified so there's not much chance of getting bored. I think it's a great lifestyle. And if you like the work you do, it doesn't matter as much about the wages. It's part of that alternative economic model. Instead of the measure of society being the gross domestic product, it's the human happiness index. So if your job brings you half the amount of money but twice the amount of happiness, which will it be? That's a big part of the benefits. It's more of a lifestyle than a job. Put the two together and $12 an hour is fine. I don't mind living on $12 an hour. Our expenses are also low because the co-op is here to support farming. We pay $340 a month per person to live here, which is less than you'd usually pay in the area. So these things balance out."

The shared approach must also take some of the anxiety of collapse out of the picture, I ventured.

"It's frustrating but important to look at economics. Frustrating because it always seems to be the economics are needed to balance out environmental ethics. The reason I left when I first came in to farming, and said I didn't want to farm anymore, was I had this ideal you could be really light on the land. I don't want to use machines on the land, I don't want to use a tractor, and I realized you can't not use a tractor very easily and still make a living, at least not on the scale we're at, and we're employing quite a few people. I didn't want to sit on a tractor and suck diesel fumes all day but I just decided to work with the compromise and one day figure out how to do it without machines. I'd like to farm without tilling the ground but I don't know how to do that yet."

Is it just a question of experience, doing it long enough until you get it right?

"I don't know. Like with anything, you're always learning. I spent eight months on Cortez with Linnea. They have a specific climate and specific soil and land and systems and irrigation and so on. Then I moved to this farm. It takes five years to get to know land. Now I know when I go out to plant which area is slug-ridden and which area is really well-drained and which area is wet. And then it's constantly changing. In five years I've never seen kale die like it did this winter. Maybe every ten years we see a drought like we've never seen before. Every season we learn something new. We're constantly responding to new environments. It takes about three years to know how to grow a specific crop, and it takes about five years to figure out how to grow on specific land.

"By *learn*, I mean get an inkling that you spend the rest of your lifetime tweaking and perfecting. I think you can learn in a year and just go out and do it. But your efficiency gets better and better. We use interns, and we've noticed that when we have them stay a second year we always do better. In organic farming, I would say 75 percent of the cost is labor. It's all a matter of working efficiently;

that's where you make your margins. You're always learning so it never gets boring. If you think you've got it all figured out, you probably haven't."

Any final tip for the home grower, something useful from the real-life farmer?

"I don't know. A couple of years ago I was talking to a farmer and he had a great crop of onions so I was trying to get the secret out of him. I asked him and he said, 'I don't know, I always have a terrible crop of onions.' I'm like, 'Well, what did you do differently?' He just sort of paused and sighed and said, 'You know what, I don't pretend to know a goddamn thing anymore. I did the same thing I've always done and they just turned out great this year, so go figure.' So, I don't know, I'd need to farm for another forty years before I can give people a tip. No, wait, I guess the tip is: just try it. I remember working in the community garden and there was somebody who wanted to plant beans in the middle of February. They were runner beans and granted they can germinate a little earlier but the middle of February is still pretty damn cold. And my first thought was to discourage it, which I kind of did, but I said, 'Well, try it if you want,' and she had the first beans of the garden for sure. So yeah, just try stuff. It's all experimenting."

Cuban model

The Cubans didn't ask to become the world's biggest experiment in urban agriculture, but when the Soviet Union imploded in the early 1990s, cheap imports of petroleum-based products came to a sudden halt. Until then, Cuba had had the most industrialized agriculture system in Latin America. It was a model similar to that seen all over North America: big farms growing mono-crops to be shipped elsewhere, with everything based on the low cost of fossil fuels used for fertilizer, pesticides and transportation.

Then Gorbachev opened the door, the Eastern bloc poured through and the Soviet Union went belly up. For Cuba, Peak Oil hit with a thud. Russian tractors lay rusting in the fields for lack of parts and petrol, while sweet deals for Cuban exports such as sugar dried up. The time known as the Special Period had begun.

The whole island went hungry. The average Cuban went from eating almost three thousand calories a day (about what we eat if we don't pig out) to less than two thousand. So where to get food? The US was growing tons of it just ninety miles away, but American presidents have all the tolerance of ayatollahs when it comes to Havana. The US actually tightened its economic embargo on Cuba in 1992.

Cuba had no choice but to grow its way out of the problem. With more than 70 percent of the population living in cities, the government encouraged urban agriculture. It ruled that any unused city lot, even government-owned, could be used to grow food. It also decided that farmers could sell their surpluses on the open market. The government provided training and technology in various organic pest-control strategies, sold tools and supplies

Havana turned a food crisis into the world's biggest experiment in organic urban farming.

in stores set up in urban areas and established markets throughout the city where local food could be sold.

The results, I had heard, were impressive. And thanks to readers of the online journal *The Tyee*, who contribute to an annual
fellowship for journalists, I got to go to Cuba to see for myself.
Tough assignment, I thought, stepping through a late December
snowbank on the way to the airport while knowing I was hours
away from floating in a turquoise sea. But someone has to do it.

I found the Cubans were indeed eating well — or at least eating
enough: cuisine is apparently not one of their strong points. The
statistic often cited is that half the fresh produce eaten in Havana
is now grown in the city, and this is meant to make everyone's
organic spirits soar, but it doesn't mention the fact that Cubans
don't seem to eat a lot of fresh produce to begin with. It's not a
salad-lover's paradise. The most popular food trend I noticed in
Havana was the microwavable mini-pizza. They weren't bad, but
after a few days I was keen to eat something local that was real.
Finally one Saturday night, famished, I found a vegetarian restaurant and could barely contain my joy. Until the waitress pointed to
the only food left in three gaping bowls inside a glass case.

"Why does the fried rice have ham in it?" I asked.

"Vegetarians in Cuba are *poco*," she said with a shrug.

At least the farms themselves passed with full marks. By 2010
Cuba had progressed beyond the Special Period of deprivation,
so I didn't see the vegetable planters on every corner or the pigs
in bathtubs. Farmers had sorted themselves out as a professional
group, with most of the growing now being done by those who
found they were good at it, and preferred it to their former jobs as
clerks or policemen or janitors. Most of the growers I met spoke
approvingly of their working conditions, and also the pay — with
a decent harvest they could easily make twice the average state
wage of $20 a month.

Beautiful as Havana was, it was a little disappointing at first
not to see a city overrun with crops. Then I began noticing more

Miguel Salcines works in the cooperatively-run Vivero Alamar organopónico in East Havana.

farms the more places I went. Slogging in the heat, choking on the diesel fumes, I would suddenly turn a corner onto a football-field-sized *organopónico*. This is a Cuban word for rows of crops grown in raised beds in areas where the soil is otherwise poor, rocky or nonexistent — a common urban situation. They use whatever they have on hand to hold up the beds: rocks, cement chunks, plastic sheeting, roofing tiles. The soil is usually introduced, a combination of compost and manure, which is then planted intensively. They try not to leave any bed empty for more than 48 hours. The need to constantly replenish the nutrients explained the popularity of the worm composting systems I saw everywhere. I also saw numerous examples of the common-sense approach to organic agriculture at which the Cubans seem to excel, perhaps not surprising given the high level of education, the lack of money to buy stuff and their decade-plus experiments in non-chemical approaches to pest control. Interplanting crops with strong-scented varieties such as marigold and basil, growing a diversity of crops in rotation and using helpful bio-predators were all scientific experiments being borne out on the land.

The highlight of my trip was finding the UBPC Organopónico-Vivero Alamar cooperative farm in east Havana, thanks to a tip from someone I met in a bus station. I didn't realize until later it was actually visited fairly often by foreign journalists looking for the good news urban agriculture story. In any event, it was a revelation.

I found it thanks to my fellow bus passengers, one who paid my two-cent fare and another who stopped reading his Noam Chomsky book to volunteer to direct me from the bus stop to the front gate. The entrance was taken up by a market area selling the farm's produce. Inside were a few white-walled and red-roofed single-story buildings, some netted-roof areas warding off the hot Caribbean sun for certain crops and starter plants beneath, and then long, red-clay rows of fresh green produce stretching off toward distant fruit trees.

I felt grand just to be there, like I'd stumbled onto the mother lode of global urban agriculture. Although, I realized, I was parched. Then an older farmhand who had been laughing with a colleague over a mound of coconuts they were pretending to husk noticed me and offered one to drink. I have never known a

Street food from street farms in Havana.

more refreshing liquid than green coconut, and this one tasted like nectar.

The farm manager was Miguel Salcines, a former government employee in the agricultural ministry and a likeable sort who insisted I ask any questions I liked. We spoke through an interpreter, a co-op employee who was also working on his Ph.D., a fact that gave Salcines his first opportunity to brag: he said that 20 of the 170 workers who make up the co-op had advanced degrees.

"We're all owners," Salcines explained. "When someone wants to join, they enter on a 90-day trial period. At the end of 90 days we have an assembly where we discuss whether they can enter or not. We do everything democratically. I'm the president, but I'm elected for a five-year term by secret ballot. We don't put business over social aspects here. We believe in social justice."

Salcines said 18 percent of the workers were seniors, which helped address a problem in Cuba where elders are often left idle or alone. He showed me some of their growing projects, including one area with a pyramid that he was convinced did something to concentrate energy to beneficial effect. I didn't bite on that one, unwilling to let any New Age detours cloud my sunny outlook. Instead I asked what he thought about the future of urban agriculture based on his experience in a world-leading role.

He denied the lofty position, insisting Cuba was still far behind, then said, "The world needs urban agriculture. We had no alternative. For political reasons, we had to do it first. Well, maybe not first if you count China. But we did it because we needed to find a way to feed people using less energy. Organic was the answer. We've only been doing it for ten years so we still have a lot to learn. So far it's working. Already in Cuba, urban agriculture is

Walk This Way

Examples & Inspiration

Here's a good reason not to skip class when the guest lecturer shows up. BTTR ("back to the roots") Ventures began when two UC Berkeley students heard a visitor say women in Africa were growing mushrooms from coffee grounds to fight malnutrition. They thought, we have a lot of coffee, maybe we could try that. They "did a ton of research, consulted expert mycologists, and watched a lot of YouTube videos about growing mushrooms." The result, as reported in the Wall Street Journal, BBC, Newsweek and other places, is a roaring business in zero-waste, do-it-yourself home mushroom growing kits that are popping up in stores everywhere like…mushrooms.

— bttrventures.com —

employing 400,000 people if you count everyone involved in the stores, administration and so on."

If the Alamar *organopónico* is the future of urban agriculture, with bigger farms managed by co-owners who use organic growing methods and understand the social value of working together, I say: bring it on. And don't forget the fresh coconuts.

TAKE HOME MESSAGE

We're all owners.

CHAPTER 10

CITY FOOD OF THE FUTURE
WHIZ-BANG OR WTF?

Here's one vision of the future of our food, from an article in *Maclean's* magazine on August 19, 2010:

> Ethiopia's biggest greenhouse farming operation is kept hidden from curious, or hungry, eyes; even in Awassa, the southern city where it's housed, few know it exists. Two kilometres down a dusty private road, past a checkpoint guarded with AK47s, hundreds of pristine, white greenhouses suddenly appear, alien to the setting. Farming in Ethiopia is still done by sickle and ox-driven plough. But inside Awassa's cool, humidity-controlled greenhouses, vines are fed by a computerized irrigation system, the latest Dutch agricultural technology.
>
> Every day, a workforce of 1,000 locals pick, pack and load hundreds of tons of fresh produce onto waiting trucks, including 30 tons of tomatoes alone. After reaching the capital, Addis Ababa, the produce is flown to a handful of Middle Eastern cities, entirely bypassing Ethiopia, one of the hungriest places on the planet. The trip from vine to

227

store shelf takes less than 24 hours. It's the latest project by Saudi oil and mining billionaire, Sheikh Mohammed Al Amoudi. And it may be the future of farming.

This may be an extreme glimpse into what some see as the whiz-bang approach to future food with unseen labs, skyscraper farms and cows in high-rises. It's based on the expectation that no matter how bad things get, some egghead will invent a technological solution to get us out of it. If we can walk on the Moon, surely we'll figure out some way to grow all our food in a test tube.

Perhaps, but history isn't encouraging on this count. In *A Short History of Progress*, Ronald Wright notes that the food of the late Stone Age is the one technology we cannot live without. The crops of about a dozen ancient peoples still feed the six billion on Earth today. Despite centuries of scientific crop breeding, despite the so-called Green Revolution of the 1960s and the genetic engineering of the 1990s, not one staple has been added to our diets since prehistoric times. As we domesticated these plants, they domesticated us. Without us, they would die, and without them, we would die. So our lives seem to be bound up with theirs forever. Maybe we'd better learn to get along with them, sticking with real food, rather than wait for the test-tube variety to save everything.

Can organic feed the world?

Vandana Shiva, an Indian physicist and advocate for small farmers, says the answer is not just yes—it's the only thing that *can* feed the world. She describes two ways to scale up production: 1) get farmers off the land and replace them with machines, or 2) put farmers back on millions of small farms. The first approach is the dominant agribusiness-run global food system we've tried and it's failed, leaving a billion hungry people. The second is the way the world will have to go since it's the only one that reduces the effects of climate change, cuts our dependency on fossil fuels, enhances our fragile biodiversity and increases employment. Then there is

Homes and food will go well together in the city of the future.

the issue of food democracy. "Only in a decentralized food system can the right to food be defended," says Shiva. "Neither the Green Revolution nor genetic modification can give food security."

A common retort from those who fail to see the problems inherent in industrial agriculture is that organic is fine, as a niche, but you can't feed the world with it. You still see a similar toss-off line in mainstream media reports that equate small farms with inefficiency, implying that only large industrial farms should be considered serious players in the fight against global hunger.

Oh really? A Cornell University study reported by David Pimental, professor of ecology and agriculture, compared organic and conventional farms over 22 years. He found organic farms producing the same yields of corn and soybeans, and more in the drought years, while using 30 percent less energy, less water and no synthetic pesticides, all while maintaining natural fertility in the soil.

The highest yields on the planet are not found on big factory farms. They're in small-scale, labor-intensive operations where people work the land, often organically. Some of them are actually in cities. Alternative agriculture can feed the planet.

Here's another view from Ethiopia to contrast with the one above.

Seleyn DeYarus, development director of the Organic Center, cites the Tigray Project in Ethiopia. "Local and national experts have cooperated with farmers in the Tigray region and tapped the rich knowledge of the farmers to understand and utilize local ecosystem elements rather than depend on fertilizers. Tigray has achieved higher yields, higher groundwater levels, better soil fertility, increased household income, and stronger livelihood opportunities for farmers than previous efforts with conventional agriculture. The Ethiopian government has now adopted this approach to mitigate soil damage and alleviate poverty in 165 local districts in the grain-producing parts of Ethiopia."

No farmer, no farm

What's the future to be? There will be food and there will be farms. We hope it will be less factory fuud products and more fresh, tasty, healthy real food.

But does it matter how it's grown? If we can do it with cows in high-rises, is that such a bad thing?

The problem with the whiz-bang scenarios is how they're typically one-dimensional, focused on yield alone, while ignoring the bigger ecological picture. That picture includes people. So whenever anyone suggests a new technology, skyscraper farms or magic protein pills, it's worth asking just how, and by whom. There's no future in farming without farmers.

It's also critical to judge these futuristic schemes with an ecological yardstick. Mark Bomford from the Centre for Sustainable Food Systems at the University of British Columbia Farm says we have to look at the inputs and outputs. "What's never been done in the vertical farming concept is a robust ecological analysis that actually looks at the larger system. Where is all the energy coming from? Where is it going? All of the trucks, nutrients, waste, every-thing has to be considered. The idea that you don't need soils and all these messy ecological things to grow food shows a complete lack of understanding of the ecological processes that support our food system and our civilization."

So, high-rise cows, maybe, they could be interesting, like any gadget. But it's still the living planet that supports us, so to think of getting food without a fundamental understanding of ecology is just plain wrong.

Dr. Evan Fraser, from the Geography Department of the University of Guelph, Ontario, told CBC Radio he hoped a scientific breakthrough can save us, but had his doubts.

"If you look at the last sixty years roughly of crop genetics and breeding, what we've tended to have done is make extremely productive crops that are very, very wimpy in terms of being able to tolerate climactic extremes or pests outbreaks or what-not. So what we've done is produce these extremely productive crops that are absolutely dependent on large amounts of water and large amounts of fertilizer. If we continue down that path of breeding for more productivity, we would actually be making less resilience in the system in the future. So it all depends on how we use our science that we've got. And the history suggests that we don't always use it to make more resilient systems."

So how *do* we feed the growing population?

"I think this will be *the* problem that defines the next hundred years. The best middle ground is   First the farmer, then the farm.

what's called the nested bio-region approach where you take a region that's got a special endowment to do something. Say it's pastureland. Where I used to live was the north of England, which is rolly hilly countryside; it's fabulous land for producing dairy and beef and lamb. That region should continue to produce dairy and beef and lamb, and we should work to get the economic efficiencies and the ecological efficiencies of specializing that region. That kind of specialization, however, does not mean they should be creating a genetically identical sheep and stamping it out every five feet across the entire landscape of the Yorkshire dales. Within that landscape there needs to be a lot of diversity. Diversity within the crops and diversity at the landscape level. Hedgerows, forests, that sort of thing. So what we need to do then is have a regional area with a lot of diversity in it but that is specialized in a particular type of crop, which then trades with other areas that are doing the same thing but with different crops. And hopefully that way we will have a resilient and productive system.

"We're also going to have to devote more of our GDP to buying food. We're going to have to spend more money on food because we can't continue to buy food that is essentially being watered with fossil fuels. That's just not sustainable. And we are also going to have to have an economy that involves more people working on food production. In terms of local gardens as well as more jobs on farms. I think the economy will ultimately shift. It hopefully will shift slowly and gradually towards that with no abrupt shocks, but I think ultimately we will see a more agrarian type of economy a hundred years from now."

The future now

Harold Steves believes the future is bright for urban agriculture. "In the last three or four years I've had as many people contact me as I did in the last twenty. The idea is growing very rapidly. I think the world is in for a surprise. People are resilient and we'll find ways to make it happen."

So for an aspiring farmer reading this, are you saying that if they're keen they can make it?

"Absolutely. The thing they've got to recognize is you don't have to be big to be good. It's hard work but it's very rewarding."

TAKE HOME MESSAGE

Plant food. Save the seed.
Pass it on.

Notes

Chapter 1

1. Urban agriculture crops represent a small portion of the global food market; *Climate-smart agriculture,* fao.org/climatechange/climatesmart/66250/en/

2. Although we may take some comfort in learning there are 800 million urban farmers; "Spotlight/1999. Issues in urban agriculture," fao.org/ag/magazine/9901sp2.htm

3. Livestock production is responsible for 18 percent of greenhouse gas emissions; "Spotlight/2006, Livestock impacts on the environment," fao.org/ag/magazine/0612sp1.htm

4. Already 90 percent of US cropland is losing its topsoil; *Cornell University Science News,* August 7, 1977, news.cornell.edu/releases/aug97/livestock.hrs.html

5. The Alliance for a Green Revolution in Africa (AGRA) may be counting on genetic engineering; "Gates Foundation Invests in Monsanto at the Expense of Small-scale African Farmers," *Signs of the Times,* August 25, 2010, sott.net/articles/show/214352-Gates-Foundation-Invests-in-Monsanto-at-the-Expense-of-Small-scale-African-Farmers

6. The other end of the spectrum includes places like Detroit; *Food and Society Fellows,* July 2010. "Detroit: The Business of Urban Agriculture," foodandsocietyfellows.org/digest/article/detroit-business-urban-agriculture

7. Latin America is rapidly catching on; "Urban Agriculture and Community Food Security in the United States: Farming from the City Center to the Urban Fringe. A Primer Prepared by the Community Food Security Coalition's North American Urban Agriculture Committee," October 2003, foodsecurity.org/Primer CFSCUAC.pdf

8. The National Gardening Association reported a 19 percent increase in home food gardening from 2008 to 2009. "Garden Market Research. The Impact of Home and Community Gardening in America," gardenresearch.com/index.php?q=show&id=3126

9. The worst recent case involved radish sprouts; "Hygiene Practice Manual for Radish Sprouts Production in Japan," FAO/WHO Global Forum of Food Safety Regulators. Marrakesh, Morocco, 28–30 January 2002, fao.org/docrep/meeting/004/x6923e.htm
10. A UC Davis Department of Agriculture and Natural Resources study recommends buying certified pathogen-free sprout seeds; "Growing Seed Sprouts at Home," University of California Davis, Division of Agriculture and Natural Resources, Publication 8151, postharvest.ucdavis.edu/datastorefiles/234-412.pdf

Chapter 2

1. MSGs (multistory gardens) are an ambitious name for the cereal sacks used in refugee camps in Africa; "Multi-storey Gardens to Support Food Security," Mary Corbett, Urban Agriculture magazine, number 21, January 2009.

Chapter 3

1. Such as: the US Department of Agriculture found the residues of pesticides in 7 out of 10 fruits and vegetables tested; foodnews.org /reduce.php
2. The world's largest cistern is the Yerebatan Saranyi in what is now Turkey; grownyc.org/openspace/publications
3. In good loamy soil, according to researchers at Cornell University, 2.5 centimeters or 1 inch of water will penetrate to a depth of 38 centimeters; vegetableexpert.co.uk/WateringYourVegetables.html
4. The Union of Concerned Scientists want you to know that as a grower you have a role to play in saving the planet by combating global warming; *Earthwise*, Summer 2010; ucsusa.org/publica tions/earthwise/close-to-home-summer-2010.html

Chapter 4

1. Fukuoka himself was a bit of an eccentric (he tried to talk the Rodale folks out of promoting composting); onestrawrevolution .net/MasanobuFukuoka.htm
2. Canadian government veterinarians say small backyard flocks are not a concern; "Keeping Backyard Hens — The Basics," Heather Haven, dailyeggs.com/Chicken%20class%20complete%2010.09 pdf.pdf

Chapter 5

1. Since the 1990s, just five biotech companies have bought over 200 seed companies; "Revealed: How Seed Market is Controlled by

Monsanto, Syngenta, Bayer, Dow & DuPont," by Tom Levitt, *The Ecologist*, October 7, 2010.

2. In this case resistance is fertile: after the Haiti earthquake when Monsanto together with USAID "donated" 460 tons of its hybrid seeds; "Haiti's farmers call for a break with neoliberalism," *GRAIN*, July 2010, grain.org/seedling/?id=694

3. As a public health service in 2007, four Canadian federal politicians volunteered to have their blood and urine tested for toxins; "Poisonous Environment: Test Finds MPs' Bodies Full of Toxins," *Vancouver Sun*, January 4, 2007.

4. Researchers recently tested a large number of Canadians' blood, and found lead in 100 percent of the subjects; "Younger Canadians have more BPA in their bodies than parents: Study," Sarah Schmidt, *Postmedia News*, August 16, 2010.

5. On the other hand, a study of 141 backyard gardens in Boston found the level of lead in raised beds *rising* over four years; "Urban Gardens: Lead Exposure, Recontamination Mechanism, and Implications for Remediation Design," Heath F. Clark, Debra M. Hausladen, Daniel J. Brabander. Department of Geosciences, Wellesley College. Environmental Research 107 (2008) 3122-319.

Chapter 7

1. Montreal now has some of the most supportive policies for urban agriculture in North America. It has an estimated ten thousand community gardeners; "A Seat at the Table: Resource Guide for Local Governments to Promote Food Secure Communities," June 2008, British Columbia Provincial Health Services Authority, phsa.ca/NR/rdonlyres/D49BA34E-B326-4302-8D0C-CC8E5A23 A64F/0/ASeatattheTableResourceGuideforlocalgovernmentsto promotefoodsecurecommunities.pdf

2. In 1965 a Tokyo housewife thought the milk in the local stores wasn't that good, and expensive besides; seikatsuclub.coop /english/

3. When we talk about "food security" we often think we're talking about the poor, such as the 800,000 Canadians who now visit food banks each month; cafb-acba.ca/main2.cfm?id=1071852 F-B6A7-8AA0-6DBD8CE5374486A9

Chapter 8

1. One study reports England losing 60 percent of its orchards since 1960; independent.co.uk/opinion/commentators/michael -mccarthy-a-celebration-of-the-english-apple-2106937.html

Chapter 9

1. It's already been described by the International Assessment of Agricultural Knowledge, Science and Technology for Development (IAASTD), a UN- and World Bank-funded study by more than 400 scientists in 120 countries; greenfacts.org/en/agriculture-iaastd/index.htm

2. Remind them what happened in Madagascar when the government there cut a deal; news.bbc.co.uk/2/hi/africa/7952628.stm

3. In Canada, farmers now take on $23 in debt for each dollar they earn; cbc.ca/canada/saskatchewan/story/2010/06/07/sask-nfu -report-farms-corporate-ownership.html

4. The average farmer in the US is said to be 57 years old; prb.org /Articles/2000/TheGrayingofFarmers.aspx

5. It's enough to say, farmers' markets: good, present system in which produce travels an average 1,500 miles before it is consumed: madness; attra.ncat.org/attra-pub/foodmiles.html

6. Hugh Joseph of the New Entry Sustainable Farming Project at Tufts University in Massachusetts compared the U.S. government's "Thrifty Food Plan" to a version featuring local, sustainable food; digitaljournal.com/article/274391

7. The average Cuban went from eating almost three thousand calories a day (about what we eat if we don't pig out) to less than two thousand; harpers.org/archive/2005/04/0080501

Chapter 10

1. Vandana Shiva, an Indian physicist and advocate for small farmers, says the answer is not just yes; "Vandana Shiva. The Future of Food," youtube.com/watch?v=vi1FTCzDSck

2. He found organic farms producing the same yields of corn and soybeans, and more in the drought years; "Point-Counterpoint on Food," from The Local Harvest, The Newspaper of Local Food in Kingston and Countryside, Volume 2, 2007.

3. Dr Evan Fraser, from the geography department of the University of Guelph, Ontario, told CBC Radio he hoped a scientific breakthrough can save us, but had his doubts; cbc.ca/quirks/episode /2010/09/18/september-18-2010/

Index

hydrogels, 50
hydroponics, 41–42

I
indoor growing systems, 40–42
industrial farm system, 17–18.
    see also Big Food
inner city farming, 158–160,
    173–174, 182, 188. *see also*
    empty city lots
Integrated Pest Management
    (IPM), 114–115
International Assessment of
    Agricultural Knowledge,
    Science and Technology for
    Development (IAASTD), 204

J
Japan, 33, 165–166, 179–181
Jean-Baptiste, Bazelais, 137
Joseph, Hugh, 207–208

K
Keating, Marie, 117–118
Kebede, Assefe, 149–150
kitchen growing, 30–35. *see also*
    confined space growing

L
lamb's quarter, 155
land use, 202–204
lawns, 82–83, 95, 131
lead poisoning, 139, 140, 141
Levenston, Mike, 29–30
lockbox, 74, 75

M
Macdonald, Cam, 132–133
Madagascar, 204
manganese, 142
Mansfield, Brent, 162–165
McFadyen, Lee, 130
meat, 17
medicines, 211

microgreens, 32–33
mites, 150
modern food system. *see* Big Food
Monsanto, 16, 136–137, 146–147
Montreal, 174–175
mulch, 50, 82–83, 111, 115, 136, 191
Mullinex, Kent, 197
multistory gardens (MSGs),
    57–59
mushrooms, 84–86, 225

N
National Center for Appropriate
    Technology, 85
Newsom, Gavin, 185

O
Obama, Michelle, 168–170, 214
oil depletion, 15–16
orchards, 195–198
organic farming
    compared to factory farming,
        77–80
    in Cuba, 222, 223–226
    and feeding the world, 228–230
    and fertilizers, 50–51
    and pests, 113–114, 118
    as philosophy, 76–77

P
PAHs (polycyclic aromatic
    hydrocarbons), 142
Park, Iinsoo, 143–144
peat moss, 52
perlite, 52–53
permaculture, 100
pesticides
    effect of use, 76, 114–115, 118
    and factory farming, 78, 79
    and global warming, 94
    and lawns, 131
pests
    and backyard plants, 104,
        113–118

About the Author

DAVID TRACEY is a writer, designer and community ecologist based in Vancouver, British Columbia. His reports on politics, culture and the environment have appeared in the *International Herald Tribune*, the *Economist*, the *Globe and Mail*, on CBC Radio and many other places. He is the author of *Guerrilla Gardening: A Manualfesto* and *The Miracle Tree*, a novel.

His environmental design company, Eco-Urbanist, works on projects from backyard farms to community orchards. A certified arborist, David is also Executive Director of Tree City, an engaged ecology group "helping people and trees grow together."

For more information, visit DavidTracey.ca

If you have enjoyed *Urban Agriculture*, you might also enjoy other

BOOKS TO BUILD A NEW SOCIETY

Our books provide positive solutions for people who want to
make a difference. We specialize in:

**Sustainable Living • Green Building • Peak Oil
Renewable Energy • Environment & Economy
Natural Building & Appropriate Technology
Progressive Leadership • Resistance and Community
Educational & Parenting Resources**

For a full list of NSP's titles, please call 1-800-567-6772 *or check out our website* at:

www.newsociety.com

NEW SOCIETY PUBLISHERS